j92 Bush, L

LAURA BUSH

AMERICA'S FIRST LADY

LAURA BUSH

AMERICA'S FIRST LADY

Beatrice Gormley

ALADDIN PAPERBACKS

New York   London   Toronto   Sydney   Singapore

First Aladdin Paperbacks edition January 2003

Copyright © 2003 by Beatrice Gormley

ALADDIN PAPERBACKS
An imprint of Simon & Schuster
Children's Publishing Division
1230 Avenue of the Americas
New York, NY 10020

Also available in an Aladdin Paperbacks library edition.
Designed by Lisa Vega
The text for this book was set in AGaramond.
Printed in the United States of America
2 4 6 8 10 9 7 5 3 1

Library of Congress Control Number 2002103426
ISBN 0-689-85366-1 (Aladdin pbk.)

CONTENTS

❖❖❖

CHAPTER ONE

A BORN TEACHER

Laura, a girl of seven, knelt on her bedroom floor. The year was 1953. In Washington, D.C., President Dwight D. Eisenhower and his wife, Mamie, were in the White House. In Midland, a small city in West Texas, Laura lived with her mother and father in a family neighborhood.

Speaking kindly but firmly to her dolls, Laura lined them up on the bedroom floor. In her mind she was a teacher, just like her second-grade teacher, Mrs. Charlene Gnagy. When Laura gave her dolls their lessons for the day, they paid close attention, just as Laura did in Mrs. Gnagy's class.

Growing up to be someone famous was the furthest thing from Laura's mind. She never dreamed of standing on a stage with thousands of people watching her. She never longed to have reporters begging to interview her. The only "audience" she ever wanted was a classroom full of children.

Laura Lane Welch was born in Midland on November 4, 1946, not long after the end of World War II. During the war, Laura's father, Harold Bruce Welch, had fought with the U.S. Army in Europe. In 1944, he came home on leave and married Jenna Louise Hawkins.

This young couple were luckier than many, because Harold lived to come home again when the war finally ended. Early in 1946 he returned to Jenna and to Texas. Harold had grown up in Lubbock, Texas, and Jenna in El Paso, but they settled in fast-growing Midland.

Midland had started out in the late nineteenth century as a station on the Texas and Pacific Railroad, halfway between Fort Worth and El Paso. In the late 1800s, the money to be made in Texas came from shipping cattle from the ranges in the West to the markets in the East.

But in the 1920s, a huge field of oil was discovered under the Permian Basin, the bed of what had been a shallow sea hundreds of millions of years ago. Midland was in the center of the Permian Basin.

By the 1920s, more and more Americans were buying automobiles and petroleum products such as gasoline. The demand for oil soared, well after well was dug in the Permian Basin, and many oil investors made big money. In 1929 Midland's twelve-story "skyscraper," the Petroleum Building, was built for oil company offices. The light brown tower was a startling height on the flat West Texas plain and could be seen from thirty miles in any direction.

Then the Great Depression of the 1930s hit West Texas hard. The price of oil crashed, and oil wells were deserted. But in the 1940s, the war spurred Midland's growth again. During World War II, Midland became the home of the Army Air Force's Bombardier School, one of the largest in the world. Pilots learned to drop bombs by practicing on the vast, empty desert of the Permian Basin.

After the war, there was a burst of prosperity in the country and a new surge in the demand for oil. Huge pools of petroleum still lay untapped under the mesquite bushes and sand of the Permian Basin. Now, with improved technology, the drillers could reach down many thousands of feet to pump out the oil. Thousands of new wells were drilled, and a forest of oil rigs sprouted across the desert. The pump jacks, looking like giant alien insects with oversize heads, labored night and day.

As the oil business boomed, people poured into the "Tall City," Midland's nickname. The good times attracted not just people in the oil business, but also storekeepers, plumbers, teachers, police officers, people to run hotels and restaurants, and all the other kinds of workers who make up a community. In 1940 only about 9,000 people lived in Midland. By 1948 the population had more than doubled.

All those new people and their families needed places to live—and that was where Harold Welch came in. His father had been a builder in Lubbock, and Harold had always been interested in designing houses. This was his chance.

Harold worked at first as a manager for a business that financed auto dealers. But as soon as he could, he began designing and building houses, and his business did well. Laura's mother helped as his bookkeeper, working from home so that she could stay with Laura. The three of them lived with their pets in a house on West Estes Avenue, on the east side of Midland. The Welches loved animals, and their terrier dog, Bully, was one of Laura's first friends.

Harold and Jenna Welch wanted to have several children, but it turned out that they weren't able to have any more after Laura. They lavished all their love and attention on their bright, happy girl. Laura's father delighted in playing with his little daughter when he came home from work. From the time Laura was a baby, her mother read aloud to her. Later in life Laura would remember how good it felt to sit with her mother's arm around her, listening to her mother's voice.

In the fall of 1950, Dwight D. Eisenhower and Richard M. Nixon ran for president and vice president on the Republican ticket. Meanwhile, West Texas was suffering from the worst drought in years. Sandstorms regularly swept into Midland from the desert like a dirty brown fog. Tumbleweeds rolled down the streets and stuck to the outsides of screen doors. Schoolchildren got used to wiping gritty dust off their desks in the morning before lessons began.

That same fall Laura Welch, four years old, started school at a private kindergarten, Alyne Gray's Jack and Jill. Texas, like many states at that time, had no public kindergartens. Some children didn't go to school at all until the first grade. But Harold and Jenna Welch felt kindergarten was worth paying for, and Laura was eager to learn. The first thing she learned in kindergarten was the names of all the other children in her class. Laura had a very good memory.

The next year Laura took ballet lessons at Georgia Harston's dance studio in Midland as well as beginning swimming lessons at a public pool in Hogan Park, on the northeast edge of town. During the baking hot summers of West Texas, swimming was a popular sport.

The Welches, like almost everyone in Midland, went to church on Sundays—the First United Methodist Church, in their case. Laura had been baptized there as a baby, and now she joined the Cherub Choir. She also attended the Sunday school, where her mother taught. Laura's life in Midland—home, school, church—was all connected in a comfortable way.

CHAPTER TWO

A PERFECT CHILDHOOD

In Midland several schools are named after Texas heroes. Two of these heroes are Sam Houston, leader of Texas's struggle for independence from Mexico, and James Bowie, who died fighting at the famous battle of the Alamo. After Laura reached the second grade, she attended James Bowie Elementary School, a few blocks from her house on Estes Avenue. At that time in Midland, parents didn't worry about letting young children walk to school by themselves. Families didn't lock their doors, let alone have burglar alarms.

"In a lot of ways I had a perfect childhood," Laura remembered later. "We felt very free to do whatever we wanted. You could ride your bike downtown, go to the Rexall Drug and get a ham sandwich for lunch."

Laura, a quiet but friendly girl with bright blue eyes under short, straight brown bangs, quickly made friends at school. Some of her good friends were Regan Gammon, Jan Donnelly, Judy Jones, Peggy Porter, and Gwyne Smith. They visited each other's homes, and sometimes one of Laura's friends would play teacher with her. Each of the girls would be a teacher, with a bedroom apiece for their classrooms.

One day Mrs. Welch noticed Laura and her friend in the hall outside the bedrooms, talking. "I thought you were teaching your classes," she remarked.

They *were* playing teacher, Laura explained to her mother. "This is what our teachers do."

Mrs. Welch laughed, and Laura had to laugh, too. Of course it *wasn't* what her teacher did, most of the time. Laura adored her second-grade teacher, Charlene Gnagy.

Mrs. Gnagy thought a lot of Laura, too. "She was a sweet little girl," the teacher remembered later. "A top-notch student, always ready and willing to please."

Along with her friends in the second grade, Laura joined the Brownie Scouts. In those days, girls didn't wear pants to school, so the Brownie uniforms were dresses. Every week, on the Brownies' meeting day, Laura wore her brown uniform to school.

After school the Brownies walked to Gwyne Smith's house for a meeting. One of their troop leaders was Mrs. Smith, Gwyne's mother. To begin the meeting, the girls chorused the Brownie Promise: "I promise to do my best, to love God and my country, to help other people every day, especially those at home." Then they would work on an arts and crafts project. There would be refreshments, such as cookies and soda.

At school or at home, one of Laura's favorite things to do was read. But she wasn't in the top reading group for her first year or so of elementary school. "I always felt slightly embarrassed that I was not in the Bluebird reading group instead of the Redbird reading group or whatever they called it," she admitted years afterward. By the third grade, though, she was reading by herself very well.

Laura had caught the reading bug from Jenna Welch,

who often took Laura to the public library in downtown Midland. The library was in the Midland County Courthouse building, on a tree-shaded square in the center of town. Across the street was the Petroleum Building, where many oil companies had their offices. Some of Laura's favorite books were *The Secret Garden,* by Frances Hodgson Burnett; the Bobbsey Twins series; and the Little House series about pioneer life, by Laura Ingalls Wilder.

Laura's mother was a calm, reassuring person, while her father was outgoing and lively. When Harold Welch walked through the door, the fun would begin. He loved to laugh, and he made everyone else laugh with him. "He tried to make people feel good," Laura said about her father years afterward.

Laura was proud of her father and his service during World War II. She looked at old pictures of him in his Army uniform, and she listened to his stories of the bitterly cold winter of 1945–46 in Germany. She was also proud of his work in Midland as a successful home builder.

Family traditions were important to the Welches. At Thanksgiving, for example, they always had pecan pie for dessert. Pecan trees grew in their yard, and every fall they gathered the nuts. Harold Welch shelled the pecans, while Laura helped her mother bake the sweet, sticky pie.

They always had sage-flavored cornbread stuffing with the Thanksgiving turkey, too. Harold Welch loved the taste of sage, and every year he would urge his wife, "Be sure to put in plenty of sage." It became a family joke, because Jenna Welch always did put in plenty of sage, without any urging.

There was only one thing about her young life that Laura might have changed, if she could have. Reading about the Bobbsey brothers and sisters or about pioneer Laura Ingalls and her sisters, Laura wished she could have a family like that. And Harold and Jenna Welch, happy as they were with their life in Midland, had always planned to have more children. At one point the Welches even considered adopting. But Laura was always their only child.

When Laura was eight, she and her Brownie Scout friends "flew up," as the Scouts said, to become full-fledged Girl Scouts. Now they could go to Girl Scout summer camp in the Davis Mountains, 175 miles and several hours' bus ride from Midland. What could be more fun for Laura than spending two whole weeks with her fellow Scouts from Bowie Elementary School?

But when Laura actually found herself at camp, so far away from her mother and father and the familiar places of Midland, she missed home terribly. Lying in her sleeping bag at night, she felt an empty ache in her chest. She asked to go home after only one week.

After all, there was lots of fun right in Midland during the summer. There was the Fourth of July parade through downtown. There were World Championship Rodeo days. And in between, there were long, hot days at the swimming pool in Hogan Park with her friends. Laura often brought Jan Donnelly, one of her best friends, back to the Welches' to spend the night.

Gwyne Smith sometimes stayed overnight with Laura, too. They had silly fun, like with Laura's tabby cat, given to her by Judy Jones as a kitten. Laura would gently push the cat's pug nose, as if that was how it had gotten a pug nose in the first place. The girls would laugh and laugh.

Sometimes Laura and her friends read together. They would take crackers into Laura's room and sit on the bed munching and reading aloud. One of Laura's favorite books was *Little Women,* by Louisa May Alcott, a story about four sisters. To Laura, the most memorable part was the scene in which Beth, one of the sisters, dies.

Laura's friends felt almost as much at home at the Welches' as Laura herself did. Mrs. Welch, always welcoming, was quick to sit visitors down at the kitchen table and pour Cokes for them. Then Mr. Welch might come in, pull up a chair, and start making everyone laugh. Marty, Laura's mixed-breed dog, would sit by her chair, wagging his tail, with his mouth hanging open as if even he were laughing.

Another interest Laura picked up from her mother, besides reading, was enjoyment of nature. As a girl, Jenna Welch had shared an enthusiasm for wildflowers and birds with *her* mother, Jessie Hawkins. Now Mrs. Welch belonged to the Midland Naturalist Group and served the group as an officer. Mrs. Welch didn't often go off without her husband or daughter, but she made an exception for the Midland Naturalists' regular birding trips.

One year Jenna Welch took her turn as the leader of Laura's Girl Scout troop. That year, besides performing community services and going on field trips, the girls worked on their bird badges. Laura, quiet and patient, was naturally good at watching and identifying birds.

A couple of years after her homesick summer, Laura felt ready to return to Girl Scout camp. This time, she enjoyed her stay in the wilderness of the Davis Mountains. She was old enough to relish adventures on her own, and by now she had a deeper appreciation of nature. Laura's love of outdoor life would remain with her as she grew up.

CHAPTER THREE

TEENAGER IN MIDLAND

In the fall of 1958, Laura and her friends from James Bowie Elementary School started the seventh grade at San Jacinto Junior High School. They joined kids from the other elementary schools in Midland, including Sam Houston Elementary. One of the boys from Sam Houston was George Bush.

Laura didn't really know George, but she knew who he was. It was hard *not* to know who George was. He was seventh grade class president, he was loud and friendly, and he was the second-string quarterback on the football team.

Also, the Bushes were an important family in Midland. George's father ran a successful oil company. He and Mrs. Bush were leaders in several Midland groups, including the First Presbyterian Church, the Midland Memorial Hospital volunteers, Midland amateur theater, and the PTA. Furthermore, George's grandfather Prescott Bush was a U.S. Senator from Connecticut.

Junior high school (grades 7–9) is often an unsettling time of life, full of sudden ups and downs and moodiness. But it seems that Laura at San Jacinto was "steady as she goes," as her father-in-law would describe her years later. Her calm, warm personality didn't change as she grew older. Other girls in her class at San Jacinto Junior High remember how friendly Laura was to everyone. She went out of her way to include girls who didn't know the other students from grade school.

And at times when Laura herself was stressed or lonely, she found comfort in reading. Her favorite way to read was stretched out on her bed. Wrapped up in a book, Laura seemed to be in a different world. She might hear her mother calling her to set the table for dinner, but she couldn't put her book down.

Often on weekends Laura and her mother drove to El Paso, more than 300 miles from Midland, to visit her grandmother and grandfather Hawkins. Laura heard the story of how Jessie Laura, her grandmother, had met her grandfather, Harold. Young Jessie Laura had glimpsed Harold, a mailman, while she was delivering milk in the family's horse-drawn wagon.

On these long drives to El Paso, or to Lubbock to visit her Welch grandparents, Laura and her mother took turns reading aloud. The trips combined things they both loved: being together, reading, and watching the sweep of Texas scenery unfold.

While she was still in junior high school, Laura decided where she wanted to go to college: Southern Methodist University, or SMU, in Dallas. She was inspired by reading a biography of Doak Walker, a football hero at SMU in the 1940s. Doak had made All-American three years running, and in 1948 he won the prestigious Heisman Trophy. He went on to play professional football for the Detroit Lions.

What impressed Laura so much was that Doak Walker had performed to the best of his ability *and* remained a decent, modest person. He was a role model, and not just for football players. Laura, too, wanted to do her best and to be the best person she could be.

In 1961 Laura started the tenth grade at the brand new Robert E. Lee High School. Midland was still growing, and Midland High School had been overcrowded for several years. The school department in Midland was eager to shift students to Lee, even though the new high school wasn't quite finished. Because the auditorium was still under construction in September 1961, Laura and her friends had to attend pep rallies outside in the courtyard.

Laura studied hard, as usual, taking honors classes and getting good grades. She worked on the yearbook, the *RebeLee*. She joined the YMCA's Tri-Hi-Y, a social service group for teenage girls. The First Methodist Church continued to be an important part of her life.

While Midland grew, Harold Welch built and sold more houses—five large subdivisions. The Welches moved to the subdivision on Humble Avenue, into a one-story, three-bedroom house with a cathedral ceiling and wood beams. Laura was proud of her father's work. Going around Midland to school, to the park, or to visit a friend, she often passed houses that he had built. It was very satisfying to look at something so solid and important to people's lives and know that *her* father had built it.

In the life of the country, the early 1960s were eventful years. On Election Day 1960, Senator John F. Kennedy won the very close presidential race over Vice President Richard M. Nixon. The civil rights movement, led by Dr. Martin Luther King, Jr., gathered force. The 1960 sit-ins at Woolworth's in North Carolina were followed by the forced integration of the University of Mississippi in 1962 and the March on Washington in 1963. The Cold War between the United States and the Soviet Union nearly exploded into a nuclear war during the Cuban Missile Crisis of 1962.

But in Midland, especially for white, middle-class girls like Laura and her friends, life was "pretty easy and simple," as Jan Donnelly O'Neill later described it. Friday nights in the fall were reserved for football games. The new high school didn't have much of a team, but that didn't stop the fans. Laura, her friends, and the rest of the student body turned out to show the school colors, maroon and white, and to cheer for the Lee High School Rebels. Pretty and friendly, Laura always had a date for the dances after the games.

Some of Laura's best times, though, were with her girl-friends. She and Regan were still best buddies, as they had been since they were nine. The two girls spent hours listening to popular songs on 45rpm records, dancing around in their socks.

At that time in Texas, a teenager could get a driver's license at the age of fourteen. Laura and her friends would pile into someone's car and go out on weekends. They might go to the movies at the Yucca or one of the other two movie theaters in Midland. They might go to Agnes' drive-in hamburger stand, a teen hangout, to drink Cokes and see who else showed up. Or the girls might just cruise up and down the streets, watching other cars full of teenagers cruise up and down the streets.

Laura's biggest adventure during her high school years was a trip to Mexico in the summer between tenth and eleventh grades. She and some of her friends from Midland traveled to Monterrey, Mexico, a historical town set in the Sierra Madre mountains. There they attended classes in Spanish language and culture. Outside class, they listened to popular Spanish songs on the radio and tried to translate the words.

So teenage Laura led an almost perfectly happy life—until one night during November 1963. It was the fall of Laura's senior year in high school, shortly after her birthday. Laura was driving her Chevy, and a friend, Judy Dykes, was riding with her. Laura drove through a stop sign—and smashed into another car, a Corvair. The other driver was thrown from his car and died at the scene.

Laura and Judy were taken to the hospital. They had only minor injuries, but they were badly shaken. And then they learned that the other driver had been killed. Not only that, but the victim was a good friend of Laura's, Michael Douglas. He had been a track star at the high school.

At the age of seventeen, Laura had to face a terrible fact. Another person—*a friend*—had died, and there was nothing Laura could do to change that tragic fact.

The whole town of Midland was stunned and grief-stricken, but no one really blamed Laura. She was not charged in the accident. Laura had to bear her guilt, though, as well as mourning the loss of her friend Mike. She stayed home from school for a week.

"I grieved a lot," Laura told an interviewer long afterward. "It was a horrible, horrible tragedy. It's a terrible feeling to be responsible for an accident. And it was horrible for all of us to lose him, especially since he was so young."

Years later when Laura's husband was running for president, the media discovered and shared this painful incident in her life with the public. Interviewers questioned her about it, and she felt she had to make some statement about how it had affected her life. "At some point I had to accept that death is part of life. . . . At that age, you think you're immortal, invincible. You never expect to lose anybody you love when you're so young. . . . It was a sign of the preciousness of life and how fleeting it can be."

About two weeks after Laura's accident, her personal tragedy was overshadowed by a national tragedy. During his visit to Dallas on November 22, President John F. Kennedy was shot and killed by an assassin. His wife, Jacqueline Kennedy, was beside him in the car at the time. The whole nation was devastated, but Texans had to suffer additional pain because the president was assassinated in their state.

CHAPTER FOUR

COLLEGE DAYS

Laura's parents had always planned that she would go to college, and they had told her so from the time she was a little girl. They were proud that Laura was a good student. Harold Welch had taken out an education policy for his daughter when she was in the first grade. Neither Harold nor Jenna had finished college themselves, but they were glad to support Laura's ambition to become a teacher.

Ever since her decision in the second grade, Laura had been set on becoming a teacher. And she had never changed her mind about wanting to go to college at Southern

Methodist University. So in September 1964 she left Midland, where she'd lived her whole life, for SMU.

Southern Methodist University was in Dallas, which was over 300 miles away from Midland. The oldest institution of higher learning in Dallas, SMU was set in the quiet, leafy University Park section of the city. Its campus of tree-shaded lawns and flower beds had traditional brick buildings and a traditional, conservative student life. When Laura came to SMU, women students were still required to wear skirts or dresses to class.

During the fall of 1964, Laura's freshman year at SMU, President Lyndon B. Johnson was running against Senator Barry Goldwater of Arizona. President Johnson, a Texan, won the election by a landslide. His wife, Lady Bird Johnson, had an important influence on conservation. As First Lady she persuaded Congress to pass the Highways Beautification Act, which helped to preserve native wildflowers. But the Johnsons would have a difficult four years in the White House as the Vietnam War grew and the protests against it mounted.

Laura had friends at college from the first day, because some of her high school friends, including Peggy Porter, were also freshmen at SMU. Not only that, but the girls' mothers were friends. Sometimes the mothers would drive together to Dallas to visit their daughters and go shopping at upscale department stores which were not found in Midland, such as Neiman Marcus.

Dallas, on the prairie of northeastern Texas, was a huge city compared with Midland. It had some very rough sections, but that didn't affect Laura and her friends. For the most part, they stayed in the safe, pleasant University Park section.

Among Laura's college courses, English classes were her favorites. She studied hard, as she had in high school, but that didn't keep her from enjoying her friends. In their spare time, they listened to records from Laura's extensive collection. The Beatles came to the U.S. in 1964, and Laura and the other girls played *Meet the Beatles,* the first Beatles album, over and over. Laura spent hours with Peggy sitting by her swimming pool, drinking Cokes and playing bridge.

Laura joined Kappa Alpha Theta, a sorority at SMU. The sorority sisters often gathered in Laura's room, "the central headquarters for fun," as one of her friends told a reporter later. "She was never one to tell people, 'I have to study, so everyone has to leave.'"

One day, in a silly mood, Laura told the other girls, "I need to practice my Miss America wave."

Her friends laughed. What was she talking about? "You just never know when it might come in handy," insisted Laura. Holding up her hand with the middle fingers together, she moved it from side to side, like a beauty queen waving to her cheering fans.

The other girls thought this was hilarious. Not that Laura wasn't as pretty or as poised as a Miss America contestant. It was just that Laura was the last person on earth to *want* to become a celebrity.

Laura had many dates in college, and some boys were interested in getting serious. But Laura wasn't. A few of these boys she liked well enough to bring home to Midland to meet her parents. But when she sensed a boyfriend was starting to think about marriage, she'd drop him.

In her busy college life, Laura always made time for reading. Books could be a wonderful escape, but they could also expand her understanding of what life was about and what was truly important. The Russian novelists, especially Fyodor Dostoyevsky, made a deep impression on Laura. She read and reread Dostoyevsky's *The Brothers Karamazov.*

During the summer between her junior and senior years, Laura worked as a counselor at Camp Mystic, in the Texas Hill Country northwest of San Antonio. Laura was a naturally good counselor, for several reasons. She loved working with children, she loved the outdoor life, and she remembered her own homesick camp experience at the age of eight. It was easy for her to be sympathetic to young campers who were having a hard time being away from home.

Besides experiencing college life, Laura and her friends were witnessing political conflict. On many American college campuses during the 1960s, students joined in a wave of protests and demonstrations against the war in Vietnam. Under President Lyndon Johnson, the United States sent more than 500,000 troops to Vietnam, spent more than $30 billion on the war, and dropped more bombs on Vietnam than they had dropped during World War II. Yet the United States did not seem to be winning the war, and more and more Americans demanded that the U.S. get out of Vietnam. In March 1968, the spring that Laura graduated from SMU, President Johnson announced that he would not run for reelection.

There were no protests or demonstrations or sit-ins at SMU, a conservative school. But Laura and her friends discussed the war among themselves. And the national turmoil worsened. The month after President Johnson's announcement, the civil-rights leader Rev. Martin Luther King, Jr., was assassinated in Memphis, Tennessee. In June, Democratic presidential candidate Robert F. Kennedy was shot in Los Angeles, California.

In November 1968, Republican Richard M. Nixon won the presidential race over Democratic candidate Hubert Humphrey. When Lady Bird Johnson left the White House next January, Patricia Nixon would become the new First Lady.

Meanwhile, after graduation, Laura was eager to begin teaching. It was the career she'd been planning for herself since she was seven. First, though, she wanted to take a trip to Europe. Laura's idea was to go camping through Europe with a group of friends. But her parents didn't think that was safe enough. Instead, they arranged for her to go to Europe with her Uncle Mark Welch, his wife, and Laura's teenage cousin.

In the late 1960s, on the heels of the civil rights movement and the anti-Vietnam War movement, came the women's rights movement. Laura didn't march in demonstrations or join feminist groups. But being a thoughtful person, she read some of the books that questioned traditional roles for women. She and her friends discussed the issues, such as whether women should be paid the same as men for doing the same jobs, and whether husbands should help with housework and child care.

At one point Laura even challenged her father about the education he had given her. He had "programmed" her to become a teacher, she told him, so that she hadn't considered other careers. For example, she could have been a lawyer.

Harold Welch reacted by pulling out his wallet. "I'll send you to law school," he offered. Then Laura had to admit that she didn't *want* to be a lawyer. She had always wanted to be a teacher, and she still did. She just wanted to make sure she was doing the right thing.

Laura got her first teaching job in the fall of 1968, in

the third grade of a Dallas public school. At last she was living the life she'd envisioned for herself, working with young children every day. She would love them, she would help them love learning, and she would watch them grow and learn.

CHAPTER FIVE

MISS WELCH

The next year, in the fall of 1969, Laura moved to Houston, Texas's largest city, on the Gulf Coast. There she taught second grade at John F. Kennedy Elementary School. Just as she expected, she loved working with seven- and eight-year-old children. They weren't embarrassed to show how they felt, and they seemed to know what was really important in life. Teaching them basic skills, especially reading, was very satisfying for Laura.

Kennedy Elementary was in a poor and mostly African-American district, and Laura was glad to teach there. Like other serious-minded Americans, Laura was disturbed by the racial inequality in this country. She looked with new eyes on Midland, the town of her happy childhood.

In the same courthouse building where her mother had taken her to the library, there had been a separate drinking fountain labeled for "Colored." Also, the bus station and the train station had separate waiting rooms for African-American people. Furthermore, the African-American and Mexican-American children in Midland had not gone to the same schools as white children. Midland schools were still segregated, in fact. They would not be integrated until the 1970s.

Laura wanted to do her part to give all children the chance for a good education. She wanted all children to feel the way she'd felt each September, so excited about going to school. Even now, the sight of a box of new unbroken crayons, or the smell of new pencils being sharpened, brought back that beginning-of-school thrill to Laura.

All children would feel that way, thought Laura, if they believed they could learn. She certainly believed they could learn, every single child. It was up to her to give them the chance. If a child in her class was falling behind, she didn't give up on that child—she'd spend more time with him or her.

Laura's students at Kennedy Elementary felt her confidence that every single one of them could learn. They loved Miss Welch, as they called her, and they could see that she loved them. She even played with them at recess. At the end of the year, the class was delighted to hear that their beloved teacher would be moving to the third grade with them.

In Houston Laura lived at the Chateaux Dijon, a large apartment complex for young people. She was happy to share an apartment with a friend from Midland, Jan Donnelly. One side of the Chateaux Dijon had a reputation as the wild side, with loud parties and late-night volleyball games in the pool. Laura and Jan were content to live on the quiet side, away from the noise.

If Laura had lived on the rowdy side of the Chateaux Dijon, she probably would have seen a certain young man her age, George W. Bush, the same boy she'd gone to junior high school with. He'd graduated from Yale University and was now a pilot in the Texas Air National

Guard, flying out of Ellington Air Force Base near Houston. In 1970 he also worked on his father's campaign for the U.S. Senate. But Laura was as uninterested in politics as she was in wild parties. She didn't run into George during the time they both lived in Houston.

As Laura taught, she began to realize that her favorite part of the job was reading to her kids. She liked that part much more than teaching them math, and she thought she was better at reading, anyway. Also, she realized more and more that learning to read was the key to *all* learning in school. Science, math, social studies—learning all those subjects depended on being able to read.

Children like Laura, whose parents read to them from an early age, had such an advantage. These children had a bigger vocabulary, because the vocabulary in books is larger than the spoken vocabulary that most people use with their children. By the time they got to school, the children who were read to were eager and ready to learn to read for themselves. Every child, Laura thought, should feel that way about reading.

Finally Laura decided to devote her career to helping children read. She would become a children's librarian.

Going back to school at the University of Texas in Austin, she studied for two years, earning a master's degree in library science.

Austin, the capital of the state, is at the edge of the hill country of southeastern Texas. Downtown, the governor's white-pillared mansion stands behind a wrought-iron fence. The mansion is not far from the University of Texas campus, landmarked by the soaring tower of Main Building.

But in the early 1970s, Laura Welch had no connection to the governor of Texas. During the week, her mind was on her courses, such as Children's Literature and Library Administration. Cataloging and Classification were also easy courses for Laura, an organized person. On weekends she often drove the several hundred miles to Midland and back to visit her parents and friends.

After getting her library science degree in 1973, Laura accepted a job as children's librarian in a public library in downtown Houston. She thought that might be a good place to meet interesting men. She did date some, but nobody she wanted to marry. George W. Bush was still living in Houston and was now working for an inner-city youth program, but the two still didn't meet.

Laura moved back to Austin in 1974, taking a job as the librarian at Dawson Elementary School. Most of the children at Dawson were Hispanic, and the Spanish Laura had studied was useful in this job. She especially loved reading to the younger children, and she got very good at reading upside down as she showed a picture book to a group. She seemed to have found the perfect work for herself.

Not that teaching was easy—it was hard work, in fact. It was discouraging to Laura that some of the third- and even fourth-grade children couldn't read, after all their years in school. As a librarian, Laura worked with many more children than a classroom teacher did. But she wanted to connect with all of them, so she learned each child's name as quickly as she could. She knew the names of all the kindergarten children, whom she worked with every day.

Laura was sometimes tired and frustrated, but she was never bored. And when she saw a student learning to read, she knew that a whole world was opening up for that child. Then she thought teaching was the most rewarding work in the world.

Meanwhile, on the national scene, the country was stunned by the Senate Watergate hearings of 1973–74. It came out that during the presidential campaign of 1972, President Nixon's staff had ordered a break-in at the Democratic Party headquarters in Washington. President Richard Nixon and his staff had then tried to cover up this fact.

After many months of anguish for himself as well as for his wife, Patricia Nixon, the president resigned. If he had not resigned, he would almost certainly have been impeached by the House of Representatives, tried by the Senate, and perhaps even convicted of "high crimes and misdemeanors."

In August 1974 the Nixons left the White House in disgrace, and Nixon's vice president, Gerald R. Ford, became the new president. His wife, Betty Ford, quickly became a popular first lady.

If Laura had been at all interested in politics, she might have been put off by the Watergate scandal and the spectacle of a humiliated president. But Laura had never had a high opinion of politics, anyway. She voted Democratic, as most people in Texas had since the Civil War.

In the presidential election of 1976, Republican President Ford ran against Democrat Jimmy Carter, governor of Georgia. Governor Carter won, becoming the first Southern president since President Zachary Taylor. Now Rosalynn Carter was first lady.

Meanwhile, Laura was happy in her work, but something was missing from her life. She was almost thirty. Most of her friends were married, including her good friend and roommate Jan Donnelly, who was now Jan O'Neill. Laura was beginning to wonder if *she'd* ever meet the man she wanted to marry.

Jan and her husband, Joe O'Neill, were living in Midland, so Laura often saw them when she visited her parents. The O'Neills wanted Laura to get married, too. They kept trying to introduce her to an old friend of Joe's, George Walker Bush.

CHAPTER SIX

❖❖❖

"HE MADE ME LAUGH"

While Laura was teaching her dolls in the Welch house on Estes Avenue, a boy of the same age was growing up a mile or so away, on West Ohio Avenue. This boy, Georgie Bush, was quite different from Laura Welch. Instead of paying careful attention to his teacher, he might be drawing an ink beard and mustache on himself to entertain the other kids. Once he threw a football in the classroom, and it crashed through the window.

Georgie didn't plan to be a teacher—or a president, either—when he grew up. He wanted to be a major league baseball player like Mickey Mantle of the Yankees or Willie Mays of the New York Giants. George and Joe O'Neill both played Little League baseball.

George had gone to San Jacinto Junior High School for one year, when he and Laura were both in the seventh grade. The next year, George's family moved to Houston because of his father's oil business. George spent his high school years at Andover, a college preparatory school in Massachusetts. While Laura was attending SMU in Dallas, George was at Yale University in Connecticut, where his father and grandfather had gone to college.

After his brief service in the Texas Air National Guard, George had gone to Harvard Business School. He received a master's degree in business administration in 1975. Then he came back to Midland to go into the oil business, as his father had in the 1950s.

George liked the idea of living in his old hometown, and it also seemed like a good business opportunity. The oil business in West Texas was booming again. In 1973 the Organization of Petroleum Exporting Countries, or OPEC, had raised their prices sharply. Americans could no longer buy cheap foreign oil. There were long lines at gas stations, President Nixon asked Americans to conserve fuel, and the demand for American-produced oil soared.

When George moved back to Midland, he found many of his old friends there. One of them was his boyhood pal Joe O'Neill, who had married Jan Donnelly. Jan and Joe often invited George over for dinner.

The O'Neills tried to get Laura and George together several times. Knowing how different the two were, Jan and Joe didn't really expect to make a match. They just thought Laura and George might enjoy each other's company.

Laura wasn't eager to meet George, though. She didn't have anything against him personally, but she knew his family was heavily involved in politics. George's grandfather had been a senator from Connecticut. His father had been a U.S. congressman from Houston in the early 1960s, then chairman of the Republican National Committee during President Richard Nixon's administration, then unofficial ambassador to China for President Gerald Ford, then Ford's director of the Central Intelligence Agency, or CIA.

Also, George himself had just announced that he was running for U.S. Representative in the election coming up next fall. Laura couldn't imagine that she and George would have anything to say to each other. She'd rather spend an evening with her parents than waste it on an unpromising blind date. However, one evening in July 1977, she let Jan talk her into coming over for a backyard barbecue. George would be there, too, as he often was.

Sure enough, George and Laura seemed to enjoy each other's company. Jan and Joe could tell, because George, who usually went home at nine o'clock, stayed until midnight. And Laura laughed a lot, that surprisingly hearty laugh of hers. Laura was impressed with how cute and funny George was. Reporting to her mother about her evening with George W. Bush, Laura said, "The thing I like about him is that he made me laugh."

The next night George and Laura got together with the O'Neills again to play miniature golf. By that time George said later, he was "smitten." The next weekend he traveled to Austin to see Laura.

Then George flew to Kennebunkport, Maine, where the Bush family always gathered in the summer. But Barbara Bush, George's mother, noticed that he made several calls from Maine to Midland. "He was struck by lightning when he met her," said Barbara. Ordinarily George enjoyed the family get-togethers in Kennebunkport, but this summer he stayed only one day before returning to Texas.

Laura wasn't the type to get "struck by lightning," but it didn't take her long to decide that George was the one. Five weeks after their first meeting, George asked Laura to marry him, and she said yes. As Laura put it, "We don't agonize over decisions. We just do things."

Many of their friends thought Laura and George were an odd match, and not just because George and his family were political. Laura was a quiet, reserved person. She loved to spend hours by herself, reading. Her favorite time of day was the peaceful hour of twilight.

George, on the other hand, never seemed to stop moving. He ran every morning for exercise. And he loved to be around other people. He kidded them, slapped them on the back, yelled across the room at them. His favorite time was party time, with everyone talking and laughing and his own voice rising above it all.

Still, George was powerfully attracted to Laura, and not just because she was pretty and pleasant. She was also smart, and he loved the way she listened to him, *really* listened. He was drawn to her deep quietness.

For her part, Laura hadn't had so much fun for a long time. George had so much energy, energy that swept her up and made her laugh, even if she didn't necessarily agree with him. "He makes life much more exciting for me," she said later. She liked the fact that he could be "slightly outrageous."

Although their personalities were so different, Laura and George shared the same values. They were both from close, loving, church-going families. To both of them, family and friends were the most important things in life. They'd both enjoyed happy childhoods in Midland. Even though they hadn't known each other at the time, they'd known a lot of the same people. Besides the O'Neills, there was Laura's close friend Peggy Porter, now Peggy Porter Weiss. She'd lived down the street from George in the 1950s and gone to SMU with Laura.

In addition to all that they had in common, Laura and George were both ready to get married. By October they were engaged. They went to Houston so that Laura could meet George's family.

The Bushes didn't know for sure that George was

engaged, and they were dying to find out. George's mother and father were too polite to ask, but his brother Jeb burst out with it the moment George and Laura walked in the door. Jeb dropped down on one knee in front of them, like an old-time suitor. "Did you pop the question to her, George, old boy?"

George, who was almost *never* embarrassed, turned red. Laura answered, "As a matter of fact, he has, and I accepted."

George's brothers and sister cheered. "We just loved her from the beginning," said George's sister, Doro. "I thought my brother was the luckiest man in the world."

The Bushes and Walkers (the Walker side of the family had given George his middle name) were all sports-minded and competitive. George's grandmother, Dorothy Walker Bush, was as competitive as the rest of them. Years ago, she'd played in a family baseball game when she was nine months pregnant—and hit a home run.

Meeting Laura, the fierce old lady put Laura on the spot right away. "What do you do?" George's grandmother asked. She meant, Do you sail? Or play tennis, or golf?

"I read," answered Laura calmly. Dorothy Bush didn't know what to make of her.

Some young women might have been overwhelmed by the large, noisy Bush family. "Chaotic," George's brother Marvin called the Bush household. "The doors were always slamming, everybody was running around and playing sports in an extremely male-oriented family." But Laura was delighted to be marrying into a family with the brothers and sister she'd always wanted. She was glad to be included in family events, like the baptism that October of George's niece Noelle. And the Bushes were overjoyed that George was finally settling down with a mature, steady person such as Laura.

After George and Laura's return to Midland, George invited Harold and Jenna Welch out to dinner. That evening, he asked for their daughter's hand in marriage. Of course Laura didn't need her parents' permission to get married, but the Welches were touched by George's gesture of respect. And they were happy to give their formal consent to the wedding.

On the morning of November 5, 1977, Laura and George were married in Midland at the First United

Methodist Church. It wasn't a large or fancy wedding for such a socially prominent family as the Bushes, or even for the well-to-do Welches. But Laura and George both wanted their wedding small and simple, so there were only seventy-five people. Laura's bridal outfit was a beige silk dress that Regan Gammon helped her pick out in Austin. She wore a gardenia corsage at her waist.

After the wedding ceremony, there was a luncheon reception at the Midland Racquet Club. Then George and Laura left for their honeymoon in Mexico. The honeymoon was short, because George needed to get back to his campaign for congressman.

Laura had quit her teaching job to move to Midland and marry George. Now she joined his campaign, although she made him promise that she wouldn't have to give any speeches herself. They spent almost a year driving around West Texas from one campaign stop to the next in a white Oldsmobile Cutlass. The Nineteenth Congressional District, the seat George was running for, stretched up the Texas Panhandle from Midland and Odessa, center of the oil country, to the farming and ranching area near Lubbock.

Laura enjoyed the long trips through the Texas scenery, with plenty of time to think and talk. This was a good way for the newlyweds to get to know each other, because they were together almost all the time. Laura came to appreciate how much work and skill politics took. She was impressed with George's political talents, his gift for connecting with people and turning strangers into friends. "He was just great, he was so terrific," she commented years afterward. "He always said the right thing."

Laura also learned the wisdom of her mother-in-law Barbara's advice: "Don't ever criticize his speeches." Driving home from one campaign appearance, George pestered Laura to say what she thought of his speech. "I didn't do very well, did I?"

"No," answered Laura as they were turning into their driveway. "It wasn't very good."

Stunned, George drove the car into the garage wall.

Laura's most embarrassing moment during the campaign came after George broke his promise that she wouldn't have to speak. He was supposed to give a speech in Muleshoe, a town northwest of Lubbock, but he had to be somewhere else. Laura, a good sport, agreed to fill in for him. She got up on the courthouse steps by herself, her knees shaking . . . and forgot most of what she was going to say. After a couple of minutes, she sat down.

But what Laura really minded—much more than making a fool of herself—was hearing George criticized by his opponents. During this campaign they called him an Eastern carpetbagger, although George had grown up in Texas and loved the state. They called him a rich boy who had never worked for his living. They accused him of trying to buy college students' votes with free beer.

The Fourth of July parade in Muleshoe was a low point of George's campaign. Laura sat beside him in the back of a pickup truck, smiling and waving at the parade-watchers (and voters). No one waved back. In November 1978, George lost the election.

CHAPTER SEVEN

THE BUSHES, FAMILY OF FOUR

After the election, life settled down for Laura and George. He turned his attention back to his oil business, a partnership he named *Arbusto* (Spanish for "bush") Energy. Laura was active in the Methodist church where she had grown up. She joined the Midland Junior League, a women's organization for volunteer charity work.

At their one-story brick home on West Golf Course Road, Laura cooked George's favorite foods. He liked ordinary dishes, such as meatloaf, hamburgers, and egg salad sandwiches. She worked on the garden, where she claimed the weeds were as tall as she was when they moved in. She organized their home.

George was naturally messy. In the days when he lived by himself, there were piles of magazines and dirty laundry around the floor, and the frame of his bed was held together with a necktie. (He didn't actually *wear* ties, if he could help it.) Laura, on the other hand, liked to have everything in its place. She even organized their books the same way books are shelved in a library. She arranged the fiction alphabetically by the author's last name and the biographies alphabetically by the subject's name.

Laura and George both liked their casual way of life, close to family and friends. Laura's father, Harold Welch, would often stop by the house to see them, or Jenna Welch would invite the young couple over for dinner. "After dinner we'd play cards—hearts—at the kitchen table," Laura's mother remembered. "Harold and George were partners and they always beat us unless we got awfully lucky."

On Friday nights Laura and George usually went out for Mexican food with Don and Susie Evans. Susie was an old Midland friend of George's from Sam Houston

Elementary School, and Don, her husband, had backed George in his campaign for Congress. Sundays, the Bushes went to church in the morning and then had lunch with friends.

Every summer Laura and George joined the Bush clan in Kennebunkport, Maine. The Bushes and the Walkers had summered on the same private point of land on the coast of Maine for generations. Besides the big house, the Bush compound included a pool and sauna, a tennis court, a dock, and three guest cottages.

The Bushes were amazed at Laura. For one thing, she ate meals in such a ladylike way. They were used to eating briskly and then jumping up from the table, ready for the next activity. But George's parents and brothers and sister sat politely while Laura slowly finished every bite. After the meal, she might take a book out to the deck to read while the Bushes dashed off for boating or tennis.

Still, the Bushes were delighted to have Laura in the family. They could see that she calmed George down and steadied him. She also didn't hesitate to put him in his place, if he seemed to need it. When George came out with one of his more outrageous statements, his brothers and sister were glad to hear Laura say, "Honey, you know that's not true."

Although she was quiet, Laura had a keen sense of humor. She appreciated her mother-in-law's witty tongue and straightforward ways, so much like George. Barbara Bush was an avid reader, like Laura, and they traded books with each other.

Laura and George were both eager to have children, but she didn't get pregnant right away. After three or four years of trying, they decided to adopt a child instead. They went to the Gladney adoption home in Fort Worth, the same adoption agency that Laura's parents had once considered. Laura and George started the adoption process, filling out an application and having their friends write letters of recommendation for them.

Meanwhile, George's father was hoping to get the Republican nomination for president in 1980. Instead, California Governor Ronald Reagan was nominated, but he chose George H. W. Bush as his vice-presidential running mate. In November Reagan and Bush won the election. The following January, former president and first lady Jimmy and Rosalynn Carter left Washington for their home in Georgia. And George's parents moved from their home in Houston to Washington, D.C.

Early in 1981, Laura and George had moved along to the next stage of their adoption process, and they made a date for the Gladney home people to visit them in Midland. Then the Bushes discovered that Laura was finally pregnant. George went with Laura to the doctor for a sonogram, which shows an image of the baby inside the mother. "Here's the baby," the doctor pointed out to Laura and George. "Oh, wait a minute, there are two babies, two beautiful babies."

George and Laura hugged, tears of joy in their eyes. Laura was not only pregnant—she was carrying twins. The next day, he sent her two dozen red roses "from the father of twins."

In spite of their excitement, Laura tried to be cautious. She didn't furnish a nursery in their house, because then she would be counting too much on having these babies. She even avoided the baby-diapers aisle in grocery stores, not wanting to get her hopes up.

Laura also took special care of herself. That summer, she didn't go to Kennebunkport for the usual Bush family gathering, because she felt traveling might have bad effects on her pregnancy. In September, Laura's doctor advised her to stay in bed most of the time to prevent the babies from being born too soon. She followed his advice.

Still, Laura developed toxemia, a dangerous condition that can threaten the lives of a pregnant mother and her child. In October she moved to Baylor Hospital in Dallas, where she could have the best medical care. The twins weren't due until late December, but by late November the doctors decided the babies had to be delivered right away. On November 25, 1981, the Bushes' twin girls were born by Caesarian section.

Laura and George named one of their babies Barbara, after George's mother, and the other, Jenna, after Laura's mother. They were healthy and a good size, considering that they were premature twins. Laura and George felt deeply thankful. "We never took our children for granted," said Laura later.

However, the new parents were bewildered a lot of the time, trying to figure out how to get the babies to stop crying. "What's the matter with them?" George would ask Laura. But she didn't know any better than he did.

Fortunately both Laura and George had a good sense of humor. She snapped a picture of him jouncing both babies and singing the Yale fight song. ("Bulldog, bulldog. Bow wow wow.") That was his idea of how to soothe a child. He caught a picture of Laura with a twin over each shoulder and one hand on her forehead, an exhausted-looking but happy mother.

They both loved the early mornings when the babies were feeding quietly. George brought coffee and newspapers into the bedroom, and he and Laura would each hold a baby and a bottle while relaxing in bed. Another favorite time was early evening, after the babies were asleep. Laura would work in the garden while George sat outside and talked to her.

The grandparents were delighted with the twins, of course, especially Laura's parents. Jenna Welch tried not to hover too much, but Harold Welch couldn't seem to stay away from the babies. He came by the Bushes' house every morning around eleven, just as Laura had gotten the twins down for a nap. "Are the girls awake?" he'd call as he came in the door. "Of course, they were *then,*" said Laura's mother.

In the summer of 1982, little Barbara and Jenna were

baptized at the First United Methodist Church in Midland. As the girls grew, Laura enjoyed reading to them, just as her mother had read to her as a little girl. For Laura, reading with the twins meant sitting quietly with an arm around each child and a picture book on her lap. For George, reading was more active. He turned the Dr. Seuss book *Hop on Pop* into a physical game. Lying down on the floor, he let the girls actually hop on him.

Meanwhile, in the oil business in Texas, the boom turned into a slump. The price of oil, which had shot up to $35 a barrel in 1980, fell to $9 a barrel in the mid-eighties. George's firm, now Spectrum 7, was about to go bankrupt when he sold it to Harken Energy.

George still had his eye on politics, although he didn't think he should try to run while his father was vice president. It would look as if he were trying to get into office on his father's coattails. In 1984, when President Reagan and Vice President Bush ran for reelection, George and Laura went to the Republican National Convention in Dallas. George's father was already planning to run for president in 1988, at the end of President Reagan's second term, and George wanted to help him win.

By the summer of 1986, George had decided to leave the oil business and work full time on his father's campaign for president. Along with this decision, he realized that he had to give up alcohol. There was too much chance that he might do or say something to embarrass his father and hurt his campaign. "He was wild when he drank too much," said Laura later.

For years Laura had been concerned about George's problem with drinking. He could be boisterous even without drinking. When he had drunk too much, he might think he was funny and charming when actually he was boorish and arrogant, embarrassing everyone around him.

Laura told him this, in her quiet way. "She can be pretty straightforward for a mild-mannered West Texas lady," said George later. She knew that George loved her and the twins more than anything, and she tried to get him to see that his drinking was hurting their marriage and family life. She left books and articles on alcoholism around where he would find them.

In the summer of 1986, George turned forty. After a hard-drinking birthday celebration with friends, he woke

Official Bush family portrait, 1989

Front row left to right: Barbara Bush, George Bush, Margaret Bush; Top row left to right: William LeBlond, Dorothy LeBlond, Neil Bush, Sharon Bush, Columba Bush, Marvin Bush, Jeb Bush, George W. Bush, Laura Bush; grandchildren scattered about.

Texas governor and Republican president hopeful George W. Bush and his wife, Laura Bush, at home in the Governor's Mansion, Austin, Texas, 2000

Laura Bush with her husband, Republican candidate George W. Bush, as they celebrate his primary wins in the U.S. southern states, 2000

Republican presidential candidate George W. Bush and his wife, Laura Bush, giving a tour of their Crawford, Texas, ranch, 2000

Laura Bush on stage rehearsing for the Republican National Convention in Philadelphia, Pennsylvania, 2000

President George W. Bush and First Lady Laura Bush dancing at the Inaugural Ball in Washington, D.C., 2001

First Lady Laura Bush and her daughters, Barbara (left) and Jenna (center), attending the inaugural celebrations, 2001

Former president Bill Clinton and his wife, Senator Hillary Rodham Clinton, at the White House with new president George W. Bush and his wife, Laura Bush, 2001

From left to right: Lynne Cheney, Vice President Dick Cheney, President George W. Bush, and First Lady Laura Bush, 2001

First Lady Laura Bush with U.S. national security advisor Condoleezza Rice (center) and Polish first lady Jolanta Kwasniewski (right) in the Presidential Palace in Warsaw, Poland, 2001

Laura Bush addressing the crowd in front of the Library of Congress in Washington, D.C., at the opening of the first National Book Festival, 2001

September 14, 2001, President George W. Bush, First Lady Laura Bush, former president George Bush, and his wife, Barbara Bush, attending a memorial service at the National Cathedral in honor of those who died in New York, Washington, and Pennsylvania on September 11, 2001

Laura Bush reading to a kindergarten class participating in the Teach For America program, 2001

Laura Bush walking with her mother, Jenna Welch, through the National Gallery of Art in Washington, D.C., 2001

up the next morning determined to give up alcohol. And that was it. Laura hadn't screamed at George or told him to shape up or ship out, but in the end she won. As her mother-in-law Barbara remarked, "Laura's quiet, but she accomplishes a great deal with quietness."

As for Laura's fortieth birthday, that November, she celebrated by enjoying an outdoor adventure. She went white-water rafting with a group of women friends.

CHAPTER EIGHT

POLITICS AND BASEBALL

The Bushes moved to Washington, D.C. in 1987, so that George could devote himself to his father's campaign for president. Laura and George missed Texas, but living in Washington had its advantages. They were near George's parents, who lived at the vice president's residence on the grounds of the Naval Observatory. Laura became closer to her mother-in-law, whom she'd always liked and admired.

It was comfortable to be so near the older Bushes that George, Laura, and the twins, now five or six years old, could drop in for hamburgers on Sundays after church.

Also, Vice President and Barbara Bush were delighted to babysit young Barbara and Jenna when Laura and George were traveling. George toured the country, campaigning for his father, and Laura often went with him.

One night in the fall of 1988, when the twins were staying at the vice president's residence, little Barbara lost her special stuffed toy. She couldn't go to sleep without her stuffed dog Spikey tucked in bed beside her, she explained to "Gampy" Bush. Her grandfather was scheduled for a big debate with Democratic candidate Michael Dukakis the next day. Still, he stayed up late searching the whole house and grounds, finally finding the precious stuffed dog.

Barbara and Jenna were fraternal twins, not identical twins. That is, they were no more alike than any other two sisters—they just happened to have been born at the same time. As they grew, the twins made a point of *not* being alike. Barbara turned out to be good at cutting and pasting, so Jenna didn't want to cut and paste. Jenna learned to ride a bike early, so Barbara had no interest in getting on a bike. Laura and George tried to discourage the girls from competing with each other and to encourage both of them to try everything.

Something both the girls liked to do, though, was "teach" their dolls. Laura watched with delight as they lined the dolls up and gave them their lessons, just the way she'd done years ago. George was delighted, too. They agreed that they had the best-educated dolls in America.

As George worked on his father's campaign, Laura got a closer look at the side of politics she disliked the most. The presidential campaign of 1988 was sometimes mean-spirited, on both sides. During the Democratic National Convention in New York, where Governor Michael Dukakis of Massachusetts was nominated for president, Texas state treasurer Ann Richards gave the keynote address. She made fun of the way Vice President Bush spoke, implying that he was not a *real* Texan—in fact, he was a rich Easterner.

"Poor George," said Ann Richards, "he can't help it . . . he was born with a silver foot in his mouth." Watching the convention on TV, Barbara Bush felt sick to her stomach. Laura was also hurt to hear her father-in-law sneered at on national TV, and George was very, very angry.

What was sickening to Vice President Bush's family was great fun for the media. Reporters jumped eagerly on

Ann Richards's smart remark. It was repeated over and over on TV and radio, in newspapers and magazines.

At the Republican National Convention shortly afterward, it was a sure thing that Vice President Bush would be nominated. George was proud to be the spokesperson for the Texas delegation, announcing the votes that made his father the Republican nominee for president.

On Halloween, during the last week of the campaign, Laura, George, and the girls went to South Bend, Indiana with Vice President Bush. Jenna was in costume as a package of Juicy Fruit, and Barbara was dressed as Vampira. The next week, George's hard work for his father paid off. Watching the election returns in Houston, the Bushes were overjoyed to hear that Vice President George H. W. Bush would be the forty-first president of the United States.

The next day they all flew from Houston to Washington, D.C.: Laura and George and the twins along with the president-elect and his wife. At the time, Jenna and Barbara were almost seven years old. Picking up the wild mood from the adults, they stuffed the plane's toilet with paper. Their grandmother, never one to stand on her dignity, pulled the paper out.

Laura was glad for her father-in-law's victory, of course. But she was also happy that George was no longer needed in Washington. After President Bush's inauguration in January 1989 George and Laura and their daughters returned to Texas. They moved to Dallas, where George became a part owner in the Texas Rangers baseball team.

The Bushes' Dallas home was in Preston Hollow, a well-to-do section of the city not far from Southern Methodist University where Laura had gone to college. The spacious ranch house had stately oaks, a swimming pool, and three fireplaces. To Laura's delight, it also had a library.

Barbara and Jenna went to a public school, where Laura served on the PTA and helped in the school library. She drove the twins and their friends in car pools, and she became involved in Dallas charity work. The Bushes joined the Highland Park United Methodist Church.

Laura also took literature classes, studying ancient Greek tragedies and the Southern novelist William Faulkner. Laura was always reading new books as well as rereading old favorites, such as the classic Russian novel *The Brothers Karamozov,* by Fyodor Dostoyevsky. "It's about life, and it's about death, and it's about Christ," she told an interviewer later. "I find it really reassuring."

As a managing partner of the Rangers, George was in charge of public relations for the team. He went to every game, and so did Laura and the girls. Barbara and Jenna enjoyed their privileges as George's daughters, sitting in the front row and sometimes even in the dugout with the players.

The baseball season began each April. At that point the nights were chilly, and the Bushes had to huddle under a blanket to keep warm. During summer the evenings were long and sweltering, and the season ended in cool October nights.

George had loved baseball since he was a boy in Little League, collecting baseball cards of greats like Willy Mays. Laura had grown up going to Little League and high school games in Midland. She enjoyed the game in a slightly different way from George. "Baseball's so slow, you can daydream," she has said. But they were both happy to spend the time together as a family.

When Laura's parents, Harold and Jenna Welch, visited Dallas, they enjoyed the Rangers games, too. The whole family would eat dinner at the ball park's private club and then go down to their front-row seats for the game. One night at the game, Laura's mother was startled to see her ladylike daughter blowing a big bubble with her gum. "That didn't look very dignified," said Mrs. Welch to Laura. "Mother, bubble gum is a tradition," explained Laura.

Besides enjoying baseball together, the Bushes were adding animals to the family. George loved animals as much as Laura did, and they'd promised the twins that when they moved back to Texas, they could have pets. Barbara and Jenna each picked out a cat at an animal shelter. They called the black cat India, or sometimes Willie, and the other cat Cowboy.

Meanwhile, back in Washington, D.C., Barbara Bush's English springer spaniel, Millie, had a litter of puppies in the White House beauty parlor. "Gammy" Barbara flew to Texas some weeks later to bring Spot, a brown and white puppy, to her granddaughters.

Laura was impressed with the way Barbara used her position as First Lady to push a cause she believed in. In her role as the president's wife, she was launching a literacy program, Reading Is Fundamental. George had her throw the first pitch at a Rangers game, which was good publicity for the Rangers. In turn, George gave his mother's cause good publicity by promoting Reading Is Fundamental during the game.

During the four years that George H. W. and Barbara Bush were president and first lady, Laura and George became familiar with the White House. They and the twins spent every Christmas with the older Bushes in Washington. Laura slept in the famous Lincoln Bedroom and the Queen's Bedroom. In May 1992, George's parents invited them to Washington to meet Queen Elizabeth II, visiting from England.

In 1989 George considered running for governor of Texas in the election of 1990 against Democrat Ann Richards. But he decided it wasn't the right time. The fact that his father was president would probably count more against him than for him. It was better for him to stick with running the Texas Rangers and make a name for himself that way. Laura, of course, approved of this decision.

President George H. W. Bush ran for reelection in 1992. George W. worked on his father's campaign team again, although not as much this time. As manager for the Rangers, it was hard for him to leave his duties.

In June, George's sister, Dorothy (Doro), married Robert Koch at Camp David, the president's retreat. It was nice for the Bush clan to have something happy to celebrate, because things didn't look good for President Bush. A *Washington Post* poll showed that if the election were held then instead of five months later, in November, George H. W. Bush would finish third. He was running against Democrat Bill Clinton, governor of Arkansas, and third-party candidate, Dallas billionaire Ross Perot.

In July, George and Laura and the girls joined Barbara Bush in Kennebunkport. The Democratic Party held their convention in New York, nominating Bill Clinton. Then the Republican convention in Houston nominated President George H. W. Bush to run again, but there wasn't much enthusiasm. Now George was seriously worried about his father's chances. From the convention until Election Day, he and Laura spent a great deal of time working for President Bush.

The economy was in a slump, and voters tended to blame the president for it. George knew that too many people thought of his father the way Ann Richards portrayed him: as a rich Easterner. Laura thought this image was unfair, and she hurt for her father-in-law. She also hurt for George, who loved and admired his father and wanted so badly for him to be reelected. And she sympathized deeply with her mother-in-law.

Laura and Barbara Bush grew closer than ever during the last months of the campaign. Barbara was a lot of fun, Laura thought, with her knack for storytelling and making clever remarks. Like her son George, she could be delightfully outrageous. That October, visiting Laura and George in Dallas, plump Barbara spoke to the Institute for Aerobics Research. "I bet I'm the first speaker you ever had whose body was made up of 33 1/3 percent fat," she joked.

President Bush never caught up with Bill Clinton in the polls. Most humiliating was the fact that the voters weren't so much *for* Governor Clinton as they were *against* President Bush. On Election Day in November, Governor Clinton became President-elect Clinton. Hillary Rodham Clinton would be the next first lady.

❖

FIRST LADY OF TEXAS

After his father lost the presidential election of 1992, George thought again about running for governor of Texas. By now, he had made a name for himself in the state as the managing partner of the Texas Rangers baseball team. He was sure he could do a better job of leading the state than Governor Ann Richards. And George thought that Governor Richards's political backing was not that strong, even though she was personally popular in the state.

Laura hadn't liked the idea of George running for

governor in 1990, and she didn't like the idea of him running in 1994. She didn't want to hear George attacked the way his father had been attacked in the last presidential campaign. In Laura's opinion, the year they'd just been through, 1992, had been "a miserable year." And if George won, the spotlight of public office would be on his family as well as him. Laura especially didn't want Jenna and Barbara, now twelve years old, to lose their privacy.

Also, Laura wondered if George had sound reasons to run for governor. She asked him some pointed questions: Did he want to run for political office just to follow in his father's footsteps? Or, worse, would he be doing it to get revenge on Ann Richards?

George and Laura traveled to Houston for the Houston marathon in January of 1993. George had been training for the twenty-six-mile race. He figured that if he could run a marathon, it would be a good sign that he had enough determination to run the grueling race for governor.

The night before the marathon, Laura and George stayed with George's parents, who had moved back to Houston from Washington, D.C. The day of the race, Laura and her mother- and father-in-law stood on the sidelines to cheer George on. "Some elderly ladies are ahead of you," Barbara shouted to tease her son. But George finished that race, and now he felt he was ready for the political race of 1994.

Since George was determined to run for governor, Laura would back him. However, she stayed out of the campaign for the most part. She gave some talks, but mainly to friendly Republican Women's Clubs. She refused to voice her own positions on policy questions—that was the candidate's role, she said. Laura did talk about education and George's plans for improving schools in Texas. Sometimes she told amusing stories about her family.

George liked to mention his wife and daughters in his speeches, too. One of the jokes he told audiences was that Laura's idea of a good speech, since she was a librarian, was "Shhhh!" Laura wasn't going to let him get away with that stale stereotype. Librarians, people who wanted everyone to keep quiet!

Laura paid George back by teasing *him* in public. She told an audience, "George thought a bibliography was the life story of the guy who wrote the Bible." George got the point, and he stopped telling the "Shhhh!" joke.

On Election Day in November 1994, Laura and George voted in Dallas. By mid-afternoon, the exit polls predicted that George W. Bush would beat Ann Richards by about six percentage points. Flying to Austin, the state capital, Laura, George, and the girls waited in their suite at the Marriott Hotel. The room was crowded with campaign workers and supporters, including Midland friends Jan and Joe O'Neill and Susie and Don Evans.

That night, when the first television network announced that George W. Bush had won the election, his hotel room shook with the cheering. The Bush family went downstairs for George's victory speech, and Laura, Jenna, and Barbara stood beside him at the podium. He spoke to the crowd gathered for the victory party and to everyone watching on television. "What Texans can dream, Texans can do." Next January at George's inauguration, Laura held the Bible on which George took his oath of office.

At first, Laura's "dream" of being the governor's wife was to keep on living as privately as possible. "I thought that cobwebs would grow on the phone," she told an interviewer. She felt busy enough with moving the household from Dallas to the governor's mansion in Austin.

Also, she had to get Jenna and Barbara settled in their new school, St. Andrew's Episcopal School.

A top goal of Laura's was protecting the Bushes' family life. She encouraged George to keep a regular work schedule, going to his office at about eight in the morning and coming home at five-thirty in the evening. He often came home for lunch, and Laura, George, and the girls spent most Sundays together.

Although George was ambitious, he loved the simple routines of everyday life as much as Laura did. Each morning George would get up first to feed the pets and make the coffee. He'd bring coffee and newspapers back to their bedroom, as he had for years. He and Laura would sip coffee while reading the papers in bed.

Just a few months after George became governor, Laura suffered a great sadness. In April 1995, her father died of Alzheimer's disease. She attended his funeral in Midland at the First United Methodist Church, where Laura had been baptized and married. She thought about the kind of person he had been.

"My daddy loved to laugh," Laura described her father later. "He loved animals. He was just one of those men who never met a dog he didn't like or that didn't like him. He was funny and he didn't take himself too seriously." George wrote of his father-in-law as "kind and wonderful. . . . I miss him greatly."

In the governor's mansion, Laura's ideas about her role as the First Lady of Texas began to change. She still didn't like the idea of becoming a public figure, but she could see that she might accomplish some very good things. As part of the celebration of George's inauguration, Laura had invited seven Texas writers to give readings of their books.

Laura was nervous about having to speak at the reading and nervous about whether she'd done the right thing, inviting these writers. Some of them had certainly not voted for George W. Bush. The night before the event, she had an anxiety dream that she was sinking in Styrofoam.

However, the readings were a big hit. They were so successful that next year, 1996, Laura founded the three-day Texas Book Festival. It was a natural cause for Laura, loving books and her native state, promoting them both at the same time.

In its first year, the festival raised more than $600,000 for Texas libraries. It was wonderful publicity for Texas authors and for reading in general. Laura decided to take the festival on as her continuing project, and to make it a yearly event.

Each year the festival opens with the black tie First Edition Literary Gala. At this fund-raising party, famous authors read to the guests, and rare books and manuscripts are auctioned. But most events of the festival are free. In several big tents on the Capitol grounds, there are book-signings with famous authors, numerous booksellers, and a children's tent with crafts projects and storytellers.

Although Laura had given up her career when she married George, she still cared passionately about teaching reading. Laura had seen how much her mother-in-law, Barbara, had done for literacy as first lady, and she wanted to do the same in Texas. Working with both Republicans and Democrats in the state legislature, Laura helped write a bill to improve early childhood education in Texas. She traveled throughout the state promoting her First Lady's Family Literacy Initiative. The resulting bill provided $215 million for programs like "Ready to Read" and "Take Time for Kids."

Laura worked at promoting Texas artists, too. She and

George displayed paintings by Texas artists at the governor's mansion and at the Capitol. Each Christmas Laura picked a Texas artist to create a Christmas card for her and the governor to send out.

Laura's new public role meant some changes in her life, as she knew it would. For one thing, she had to get dressed up more than she wanted to. Her favorite clothes, jeans and T-shirts, wouldn't do. She had a Dallas designer, Michael Faircloth, make her a wardrobe of suits and dresses in a simple and conventional style.

Also, Laura worked at becoming a more effective speaker. She had never planned to give speeches, but if she was going to do it, she wanted to do a good job. She learned her lines beforehand and practiced delivering them. She began to realize that her greatest asset when she spoke for education and reading was that she really believed what she was saying. Audiences were impressed with Laura's sincerity.

When the public life got to be too much for Laura, she sometimes took refuge with one of her close friends in Austin, such as Regan Gammon. She'd call Regan and say, "I'm coming over." Then for a while, she could relax with her old friend and be just Laura, the way they'd been together when they were girls growing up in Midland. Often one of Laura's friends would join her for a long walk along the Colorado River, which runs through Austin.

Laura liked to be outside in all seasons. As a fiftieth birthday present to herself in 1996, Laura went on another river rafting trip with friends. Regan Gammon was along on this vacation in Utah, and so was Peggy Porter Weiss. Three years later, Laura even took her mother on a bird-watching trip in Belize, in Central America.

A refuge for all the Bush family was the ranch they bought near Crawford, in central Texas. Almost 1,600 acres, the ranch gave the family privacy to hike, fish, and relax. It was an excellent place for long walks and birdwatching, which Laura loved. The hundreds of acres of woods on the ranch were a good place to spot birds, such as the golden-cheeked warbler, rare outside central Texas.

Here the Bushes could spend time with each other, their dog, and maybe a few friends. The house on the lake was small but comfortable, with lots of books. George liked to grill hamburgers, one of his favorite foods, for everyone.

By now Jenna and Barbara Bush were teenagers. They were still close to their parents, but they had normal teenage ideas about how they wanted to live their lives. They became less enthusiastic about going off to the ranch with their parents, and preferred spending more time with friends in Austin. They made fun of Laura's practical, never-a-hair-out-of-place hairstyle.

Barbara and Jenna did not want to be known as the governor's daughters. Having been the president's granddaughters when "Gampy" Bush was in the White House, the girls had a good idea how unpleasant publicity could be. They used to clink their milk glasses together in a toast, "No comment," as if they were brushing off reporters.

Laura and George meant to protect their daughters, but they had yet to learn how easy it was to violate the twins' privacy. While George was still governor-elect, the family had an experience that taught them a lot. A TV station filmed a feature story that showed George, Laura, and the girls decorating their Christmas tree.

During the filming, forgetting that his every remark would be heard by the television audience, George teased Jenna about her boyfriend. Jenna stamped her foot and yelled, "Dad!" Of course her response, too, was enjoyed by TV viewers. After that, Laura and George made an extra effort to keep the girls out of the public eye. They never used them in political advertisements, and they never asked them to go to political events. They also asked the media in Texas to give their children privacy.

The twins decided for themselves to go to the public high school in downtown Austin, rather than continuing private school. They watched some TV programs their parents didn't approve of, such as *Beverly Hills 90210,* a prime time soap opera for teenagers dealing with some controversial issues. Laura sometimes walked into the room while the twins were watching the program and reminded them, "These are not our values." But she didn't make them turn it off.

Laura was glad that Barbara's and Jenna's friends seemed to like gathering at the governor's mansion. It was a welcoming place, for animals as well as people. During the years that George was governor, a new cat joined the family. Spot and George found a stray one day on the grounds of the mansion. This cat had six toes on each foot, making his paws look like baseball gloves. Laura remembered that the famous author Ernest Hemingway also had a cat with six toes, so the family named the new cat "Ernie."

George ran for reelection as governor of Texas in 1998. By this time, there was talk that he was also planning on running for president of the United States in 2000. That election seemed like a good chance for a Republican conservative to get into office. President Clinton was in disgrace, in the headlines all year for misconduct with a White House intern. Vice President Al Gore would most likely be nominated by the Democrats to run for president, and George thought he could beat him.

George and his campaign team also thought that Laura would be a great asset to him in this race. In her years as governor's wife, she'd gotten confident about standing at a microphone in front of a crowd or having TV lights and cameras aimed at her. She didn't seek publicity for herself, and this came across in her public appearances. People saw her as sincere and appealing.

During Bill Clinton's presidency his wife, Hillary, had been much criticized for taking an active part in her husband's administration. Laura was a more conventional wife, staying in the background, yet she had accomplished a great deal for reading and literacy as First Lady of Texas. She had also promoted Texas as a state with a long history of gifted authors and artists. Many people thought Laura Welch Bush was the all-time best governor's wife of Texas.

CHAPTER TEN

ELECTION 2000

Yet again, Laura had long discussions with George about whether he really should run for president. "She may seem like a quiet, retiring type," George told an interviewer later, "but she's pretty tough, tough in a good way." Living in the governor's mansion in Austin was public enough, Laura thought. Living in the White House, she pointed out, would be a whole different level of publicity.

At least as governor's wife, Laura had been able to walk out the door of the governor's mansion and go for a stroll by herself. She could meet a friend for lunch at a restaurant in Austin without having it reported on the news. But once George announced that he was running for president, Secret Service agents, who protect presidential candidates and their families, would have to escort her. And if Laura became the president's wife, she'd need a motorcade just to go to the store.

Jenna and Barbara Bush didn't like the idea of their father running for president any better than Laura did. During the election year, 2000, the twins would graduate from high school and go off to college. They didn't want a herd of reporters spying on them, using every detail of their lives for national gossip. They didn't want to be shadowed by the Secret Service for their four years in college. However, it was somewhat reassuring that Chelsea, President Clinton's daughter, had been able to live a fairly private life while he was in office.

Although Laura didn't relish the idea of stepping into the national spotlight, she thought she could stand it. What she really dreaded was seeing George criticized and made fun of, as his father had been in 1992. "There was an image out there that was not him," she explained in an interview. "You don't like to see someone characterized in a way that you know they're not."

Furthermore, if George did become the forty-third president, Laura worried about what would become of the Bushes' family life. Being governor of Texas was demanding enough, but at least George had been able to keep a regular workday. Evenings and weekends had been reserved for family, except when something urgent came up. Being president of the United States, the most powerful nation in the world, would demand much, much more of George.

In the end, Laura had to respect George's reasons for running. He thought he could change the direction of the country for the better. And he wanted to restore honor to the presidency, which he felt had been dishonored by President Clinton's behavior in office. He believed that this was the right time for him to run, and Laura knew he had an excellent sense of timing.

Early in 2000 George hit the campaign trail, and Laura traveled with him. So did Secret Service agents, who gave Laura the code name "Teacher." The first primary elections were in Iowa and New Hampshire. Speaking in Iowa, Laura criticized President Clinton, although she didn't mention him, by the way she praised her husband. Americans, she said, wanted a president they could trust to make them proud, rather than embarrassing them. "Governor Bush has represented Texas with dignity and honor," she said with her hint of Texas twang. "I'd love to see him do the same thing for our nation in its highest office."

George realized that Laura was campaigning only because she loved him and wanted to support him, and he appreciated it. His voice became hoarse with emotion as he told an interviewer that spring, "I know she's making a huge sacrifice."

One group who especially enjoyed watching Laura Bush campaign were her former sorority sisters at SMU. They remembered how years ago Laura Welch, in a silly mood, had practiced her "Miss America wave" for them. "You never know when you're going to need it," Laura had declared. And now there was Laura on television, getting into a car or stepping out onto a stage—doing her Miss America wave!

Although she accepted publicity for herself, Laura

made a point of protecting her daughters. When she heard that a *Newsweek* reporter had found out Barbara's SAT score, she called and asked *Newsweek* not to publish it. "Barbara would be so embarrassed," she said.

Laura's mother-in-law, Barbara, was a great support to her in this campaign, and sympathized about the difficulties of being a politician's wife. Mrs. Bush had had to deal with the campaign staff telling her to dye her white hair and lose weight. (She refused.) She'd learned to handle reporters who tried to get her to admit she disagreed with her husband on some issues. She was skilled at protecting her family's privacy.

Mrs. Bush also gave Laura some helpful tips on campaigning. She advised her to wear colorful clothes in public, instead of the neutral colors, like beige, that Laura usually chose. She also explained that when several candidates' wives were speaking at a campaign event, Laura could make the strongest impression by going first. And Barbara's overall philosophy of the political life agreed perfectly with Laura's: "You can either like it or not, so you might as well like it."

Laura never developed her mother-in-law's knack of

saying unpleasant things about political opponents in the best possible way. She left it to Mrs. Bush to remark that if Laura ended up in the White House, she wouldn't be like the present first lady, Hillary Clinton. "I think she would rather make a *positive* impact on the country," explained Barbara innocently.

Interviewers sometimes encouraged Laura to criticize Hillary, but she ducked the issue. "I have a favorite first lady and it's my mother-in-law," she responded. Hillary was running for an office herself that year, Laura pointed out, so it made sense that Hillary was behaving like a candidate rather than like a first lady. "You probably won't see me run for office," she said with her humorous way of understatement.

However, Laura did continue to criticize Bill Clinton by the way she talked about George W. Bush. "I think my husband will bring dignity to the office," she said. The unspoken message was that President Clinton had brought shame to the White House, and that Vice President Al Gore was tainted by his association with the Clinton scandals.

Knowing how much Laura would hate the attacks on

him, George tried to enforce what he called a "news media blackout." The family shouldn't pay attention to what was said about him in the media. They should let his campaign staff worry about that. Laura ignored this rule, scouring the newspapers and magazines for anything written about George. In fact, she sometimes read him insulting passages just to tease him.

"Bushie," George joked back, "you've penetrated the news blackout." George and Laura had had many nicknames for each other over the years, and lately they were both calling each other "Bushie." Laura used the nickname during the campaign to warn George when she thought he was being too loud and arrogant. "Bushie," she would say quietly, her voice rising at the end of the word. George would then know he should tone it down.

Much of the time, Laura would tell the media bland, pleasant things that didn't reveal anything. If an interviewer asked her how she felt about campaigning, she'd say it was "really fun," or "lots of fun." People might think from these comments that she was a boring person, but she didn't care. She was more interested in keeping her private feelings private.

In September 1999 at a memorial service for seven people shot in a Fort Worth church, Laura had been deeply moved. Many people in political life would let themselves be seen crying, to appear sympathetic on TV. But typical of her usual reserve, Laura kept her sunglasses on through the service, only lifting them a little to dab her tears away with a tissue.

Taking part in a presidential campaign is something like being picked up by a tornado. But Laura was determined not to let it *completely* take over her family's life. Jenna and Barbara needed their mother's special attention during the summer of 2000. They were going off to college, Barbara to Yale and Jenna to the University of Texas at Austin. Also, the Bushes were building a new vacation home on their ranch in Crawford, and Laura wanted to supervise the work.

Laura was also determined not to step outside her role as she saw it. As a candidate, George spoke over and over about his stand on various policies, such as gun control and abortion. No matter how often reporters asked Laura about *her* views, she refused to comment. "I'm not George's adviser. I'm his wife." When a reporter tried to get her to say how she felt about the death penalty, she countered with, "If I differ with my husband, I'm not going to tell *you* about it."

Still, George relied on Laura in several ways. He thought she had excellent judgment about people, and he listened carefully to her comments on speeches he was going to give. His campaign staff felt that Laura had a good instinct for how well George was getting his message across. Perhaps most important, having Laura beside him calmed George down and made him comfortable, even in the middle of the campaign whirlwind. When Laura urged George to appear on *Oprah* in September, he did. His numbers in the polls went up.

Just as Laura feared, George was attacked mercilessly. On the Internet his opponents spread around a group of pictures titled "Curious George," showing George with various facial expressions and an ape making similar faces. They made fun of him for carrying his favorite feather pillow along on campaign trips.

The media also noticed and reported every time George misspoke, which was often. They pounced with glee when he promised to improve the economy by "making the pie higher," or when he referred to Greek people as "Grecians." One of his most embarrassing bloopers came out when he spoke on the need for higher standards in American education: "Rarely is the question asked: Is our children learning?" Many commentators wondered why Governor Bush hadn't learned enough grammar to say it correctly: "*Are* our children learning?"

Like her mother-in-law, Barbara, Laura learned to allow reporters glimpses of the Bushes' private lives without giving away anything important. On one of the campaign trips, a reporter asked Laura if she had any advice for her husband. She looked across the aisle at George and said, "Don't smack your gum." It really did annoy Laura when George smacked his chewing gum, and she didn't mind who knew that, and neither did George. It was a harmless little personal detail for reporters to put in their articles.

Just as everyone expected, the Democratic convention in July nominated Vice President Al Gore as their candidate. At the end of the month, it was certain that the Republican convention in Philadelphia would nominate George W. Bush. Laura was to give the first big speech of the convention. This would be a far cry from Muleshoe, Texas, in 1977.

"I get butterflies a little bit, thinking about it," Laura admitted to a reporter. This would be a test of her calm temperament, facing the thousands of delegates at the convention as well as the TV cameras carrying her image and voice to millions of viewers.

To add to the stress, in an interview the day of her speech, CBS's Ed Bradley asked Laura about the tragic car accident she'd had in high school. "Can you share with us how that affected your life?"

This incident, possibly the most painful of Laura's life, had nothing to do with whether her husband should be president or not. But she answered patiently, "Of course that affected my life, in a profound way." She added, "It made me very protective of my own children. It made me realize how temporary life is or can be." Then maybe Laura ran out of patience with interviewers who wanted her to "share" her most private feelings on national television. "I really do not talk about it, and I'm not that comfortable talking about it."

In spite of all the pressure on her, Laura walked out on the stage in her lime-green suit to give her fifteen-minute speech with poise and warmth. She began by cutting off the prolonged applause with, "All right, now, quiet down," in a firm but pleasant tone, as if she were talking to her second-grade class again. She reminded the audience of what Governor Bush had done for education in Texas and how he had been able to work well with Democrats as well as Republicans. She talked about how much education had always meant to her, from the time she lined up her dolls on her bedroom floor and gave them their lessons.

After the speech, commentators remarked that Laura made exactly the right impression. She appealed especially to married women with children, a group of voters who might easily go for Al Gore instead of George Bush. Without ever mentioning Hillary Clinton, Laura was a clear contrast to President Clinton's wife, who had taken a more prominent role in her husband's administration.

During the last few months of the campaign, the race was very close. It was the closest presidential election, in fact, since the Kennedy-Nixon race of 1960. Now that the twins were settled at college, Laura threw herself into campaigning. A few weeks before the election, Laura and her mother-in-law, Barbara, went on a tour called "W Stands for Women." The point was to appeal to women voters, who were dubious about George Bush. George did gain appeal among married women with children, and it seemed that Laura deserved credit for that gain.

On election night the Bushes, including George's father and mother and his brother Jeb, and Laura's mother sat down for dinner in an Austin restaurant. While they were eating, they got some bad news. It seemed that Florida, the state where Jeb was governor, was going for Vice President Gore. This was so upsetting that the group left the restaurant and went back to the governor's mansion to watch the returns in privacy.

All through that night the election was in doubt. The TV networks declared the election first for the Democrats, then the Republicans. Al Gore called George to concede the election—and then two hours later called to take back his concession. The vote in Florida, the deciding state, was too close to call, so there would be a recount. The Democrats decided to contest the election, and the court battles went on for weeks.

❖❖❖

CHAPTER ELEVEN

LAURA WELCH BUSH, FIRST LADY

Throughout the tense time while the election of 2000 was up in the air, Laura remained calm. Her father-in-law, George H.W. Bush, spoke admiringly about the way she helped the whole family stay calm "during those thirty-five awful days when the election was up in the air. It was a savage, horrible period. But she never got rattled, never got vindictive."

In Laura's view, she and George and his team had done all they could, and now the result was out of their hands. The best things in their lives would still be there, whether George won or lost. One of these things was their ranch, where the new house was almost finished. The Bushes spent much of the time there while the election was undecided. Fortunately there was also now Laura's new dog, a black Scottish terrier puppy from New Jersey governor Christie Whitman, for them to enjoy.

Finally, in mid-December, the Supreme Court decided the election. Al Gore conceded on the evening of December 13. The Bush family began calling former president Bush, the forty-first president of the United States, "forty-one" and George W. Bush "forty-three." And Laura Welch Bush was the first lady–elect.

But even on that momentous day, Laura Bush continued to focus on what *she* thought was important. As Honorary Chair of the Texas Book Festival, Laura went to a two-hour meeting on last year's festival. Her committee members were amazed that she even came to the meeting, and more amazed at how calm and attentive she was. Only when the meeting broke up did Laura leave to join her husband—to accompany him as he delivered his victory speech.

On Christmas Day, as if the year hadn't been eventful

enough, Jenna Bush was stricken with appendicitis. She was rushed to the hospital, Laura by her side, surrounded by Secret Service agents. After Jenna's appendix was successfully removed, Laura stayed overnight in the hospital with her. To the country Laura was the first lady–elect, but to her daughters she was *Mama*.

On January 20 Laura stood beside George on the steps of the Capitol as he took the oath of office. It was an overcast, damp day, but George didn't seem to notice. As for Laura, she was especially happy that her second-grade teacher, Mrs. Charlene Gnagy, had come to the inauguration.

That night Laura dressed in a long red dress of beaded Chantilly lace for the many inaugural balls she and the president had to attend. Her friend Michael Faircloth of Dallas had designed that gown for her. As the custom was, Laura would donate her gown to the Smithsonian Institution's collection of First Ladies' gowns.

Everyone who interviewed Laura Bush wanted to know what kind of first lady she would be. "I think I'll just be Laura Bush," she answered over and over. Laura added that the first lady she admired most was her mother-in-law, Barbara Bush, with her campaign for literacy.

Another president's wife whom Laura thought highly of was Lady Bird Johnson. Laura reminded people that Mrs. Johnson helped launch the environmental movement in this country. "If you look back," Laura noted, "you see that the first ladies tended to focus on just a few issues [for example,] Lady Bird Johnson with wildflowers and highway beautification. What a lasting impact that has on the country. And the first ladies were generally more successful than their husbands. Their husbands had to deal with every issue, and so their legacy is more mixed."

When Laura moved to Washington from Austin, she brought hardly any furniture. She loved antiques, and the White House was already full of beautiful pieces with historic meaning. Laura admired Jacqueline Kennedy's good taste in restoring the White House in the 1960s.

However, Laura had no intention of becoming a fashion leader like Mrs. Kennedy. Even before President Bush's inauguration, when Laura paid the traditional formal visit to outgoing first lady Hillary Clinton, she got a taste of how her clothes would be scrutinized. Style columnists called her purple plaid suit dowdy, contrasting it unfavorably with Mrs. Clinton's stylish black pantsuit. They also criticized Mrs. Bush's sensible shoes. But Laura held to her own ideas of how she wanted to dress, no matter what fashion experts thought.

During the campaign of 2000, the media had started calling Laura Bush the "Un-Hillary," as she was a clear contrast to President Clinton's ambitious wife, the now senator-elect from New York. When Hillary Clinton became first lady in 1993, she'd made a point of moving her office from the East Wing of the White House, where first ladies have traditionally worked, into the West Wing. The West Wing houses the executive offices of the president, and Mrs. Clinton intended to take part in making policy. Laura moved her office back to the East Wing, signaling that she did *not* intend to take part in official decision making.

However, Laura intended to make a difference as first lady. There was a shortage of teachers in many parts of the country, and Laura knew well how important good teachers were to children. One program she supported was "Troops to Teachers," which encouraged men and women retiring from the armed forces to go into teaching. She even planned to go into schools and do some substitute teaching herself, to lead by example.

Laura especially wanted to improve early childhood education. She hoped that President Bush would add a reading curriculum to Head Start. "If you've been read to," she explained to TV host Oprah, "you start school with a great vocabulary." She wanted all the children in the country to have the same advantage that she'd had as a young child, with her mother reading to her every day.

Following up on the success of the Texas Book Festival, Laura planned the first-ever National Book Festival held in Washington, D.C., in September. She invited more than seventy authors. The fair would raise public awareness about books on an even larger scale than the Texas Book Festival.

All her life, Laura Welch Bush had always worked to do a good job, whatever she was doing. As a Brownie Scout, she followed the troop leader's directions and put together the best craft projects. As a second-grade teacher, she strove to teach every single child in her class.

Now Laura intended to do a good job as first lady, including some parts of the job that went against her grain.

She didn't enjoy formal entertaining, and neither did George. When he was governor of Texas, they'd somehow managed to avoid giving any black-tie parties. But in the White House, the public side of their life would have to be more formal. "People expect those who live in the White House to treat it with dignity and to be dignified themselves," said Laura.

The way Laura looked in public was more important than ever, and she planned for that in her usual organized way. In her closet, shoes were arranged by color. She labeled sets of clothes so she could remember when and where she'd worn that outfit. She kept her hairdo short and simple, and she used inexpensive Cover Girl makeup, as she had for years.

Laura understood that interviews were a necessary part of her duties as the president's wife. The American public had a right to get a look at the First Lady. Also, an appealing public image for her would help her husband politically. Laura thought talking about herself was boring, but she graciously received reporters at the White House and answered their questions.

But Laura would not allow the national spotlight to

take over her life, or her family's life. During the first month of the George W. Bush administration, she spent half her time at the Bush ranch in central Texas. The new house was finished, but it still needed to be decorated and stocked with supplies. Regan Gammon helped Laura shop for antiques and plan plantings of native wildflowers on the grounds.

An oak-lined driveway led to the Bushes' large, new one-story house, which was built for the hot, dry Southwestern climate. The facade was Texas limestone, and the slightly curved structure was only one room deep, so that the breezes could blow through. To conserve energy, the house would be heated and cooled by groundwater.

Laura had made sure to include in the new house all the things that George wanted: comfortable sofas, a comfortable bed, a comfortable shower. There was a bedroom apiece for Jenna and Barbara, when they were home on vacations from college. And there was lots of bookshelf space for lots of books.

Near the house was a pond, newly dug and stocked with bass. There was a swimming pool for the twins, and a large patio where Laura could relax in her favorite clothes, jeans and sneakers, with Spot and Barney. There was a screened breezeway where the Bushes could eat dinner with friends *or* with important state visitors. In November 2001 they entertained Russian President Vladimir Putin and his wife Lyudmila.

When they were in Washington, Laura was glad that some of their family lived nearby. She got together regularly with George's sister, Doro Bush Koch, and with Margaret Bush, the wife of George's brother Marvin.

One thing Laura and George had always agreed on was the importance of family and friends, loyal, longtime friends—people such as Jan and Joe O'Neill. "Good, solid friends," as President Bush explained to an interviewer. "They were friends before I was president, and they'll be friends after I'm president."

Laura could count on her friends not to talk to the news media about her daughters. But she could no longer count on the media to respect the girls' privacy. At the beginning of 2001, Barbara and Jenna tried to buy alcoholic drinks at a restaurant in Austin, where the legal drinking age is twenty-one. Both girls were issued citations (summons to appear in court) for their misdemeanors.

If the twins had been the daughters of an ordinary citizen, no one would have paid any attention to the incident. But since they were the president's daughters, it was a front-page story all over the world. Even though the Bushes had vowed to steer the girls clear of being involved, they realized the whole family became involved when George was elected.

On the other hand, Laura and her family had some wonderful experiences *because* they were related to the president of the United States. Laura and her mother toured the Holocaust Museum in Washington and went to the Remembrance Day ceremonies, honoring the victims of the Nazi concentration camps. It was an emotional occasion for many, but Laura and her mother were surprised that it had a special significance for them.

"I didn't know beforehand that during the ceremony they would present a flag of the United States to each of the U.S. Army companies that liberated concentration camps," Laura told a reporter. "My dad's company, the 104th Infantry, had liberated Nordhausen." When Laura and her mother heard Harold Welch's company announced and saw the flag of his division, they shed tears of pride for their father and husband.

In April 2001, Laura invited a group of friends from her Austin garden club, including Peggy Porter Weiss and Regan Gammon, to the White House. When they arrived, they found the same old Laura. On the Truman Balcony, with its awe-inspiring view of the South Lawn and the Washington Monument and Jefferson Memorial in the distance, Laura chatted and laughed, her shoes off and her dogs in her lap. They all stayed up late talking in the White House solarium, wearing pajamas as if they were ten-year-olds at a sleepover party.

That summer, an interviewer asked Laura if she still had time to read, now that she was first lady. "I read every single night," said Laura. "The president and I both read every night before we go to bed." She read old favorites and new books, biographies, serious literature, and mystery novels. The president, she said, preferred books about history or political biographies.

Even in the White House, with all the heavy responsibility that goes with the presidency, Laura and George managed to have fun. "I think his jokes are the funniest," she told a reporter. "I'll always keep laughing at his jokes." And she could make him laugh, too.

One day Laura, showing some visitors around, stopped outside the Oval Office. She wanted to introduce them to the president, but he was busy with other visitors who had overstayed their time. To give George and his guests a hint, Laura tied a note to the collar of Barney, her Scottish terrier, and sent him into the Oval Office. From outside the door, Laura could hear George laughing as he noticed the dog and the note.

CHAPTER TWELVE

❖❖❖

STEADY FOR OUR COUNTRY

The morning of September 11, 2001, was sunny and clear in Washington. In Laura's role as first lady, things were going well. Today she was scheduled to testify before the Senate Education Committee on early childhood education. That would make her the fourth first lady to testify before a senate committee.

A poll released in August showed Laura's approval rating at 64 percent, three points higher than her husband's rating. With Laura's leadership, the first National Book Festival had been held in the Library of Congress and the grounds of the Capitol on September 8. Laura was looking forward to substitute teaching this fall, as part of the Teach for America program.

On September 11, Laura Bush left the White House shortly before nine A.M. to go to Capitol Hill. As she got into the car, she heard a disturbing piece of news: a plane had flown into the north tower of the World Trade Center in New York. No one knew how it had happened, but most people thought it must be a freak accident. Then another piece of news changed the picture: a second plane had crashed into the south tower of the Trade Center. This was no accident. It was an attack.

At the Capitol Laura and her staff joined Senator Edward Kennedy of Massachusetts, the head of the education committee. They made statements to the reporters who were covering the senate meeting. "Our hearts and our prayers go out to the victims of this act of terrorism," said Laura. Typical of her, she was especially concerned for children. "Parents need to reassure their children everywhere in our country that they're safe."

President Bush, who was in Sarasota, Florida, was preparing to go on television. But first he called Laura, and they both drew comfort from hearing each other's voice. Only minutes after the president's announcement of "an apparent terrorist attack on our country," a third plane hit the Pentagon. At this point, the Secret Service ordered the evacuation of the Capitol and the White House, because they were concerned those buildings might be attacked in the same way.

Secret Service agents whisked Laura and her staff away to a secure location. She called both her daughters, then her mother. She knew they'd worry about her, and she wanted to let them know she was safe. Laura also knew she'd be reassured by talking to her mother, who had lived through the attack on Pearl Harbor at the beginning of World War II.

Meanwhile President Bush was aboard Air Force One, not to return to Washington until late that afternoon. Laura must have been worried about her husband, but she comforted the young women with her. "Some of them just fell apart and wept all day," she said.

Like the rest of the nation, Laura and her staff spent the day watching the horror unfold on television. The South Tower of the World Trade Center collapsed, 110 stories crumbling into rubble. A hijacked plane, perhaps intended to strike the White House, went down instead in Shanksville, Pennsylvania. The North Tower of the World Trade Center, also 110 stories high, collapsed. Terrified refugees fled lower Manhattan and its ballooning cloud of smoke and dust.

Thousands of workers in the Trade Center were certainly dead, crushed by hundreds of tons of shattered concrete and mangled steel. It was the worst civilian disaster in American history. The attack was also a savage blow to American pride, wiping out the tallest buildings in New York City's famous skyline and wounding the Pentagon, command central for the U.S. military.

The very next day, Laura accompanied President Bush to the Walter Reed Army Medical Center to visit badly burned survivors of the attack on the Pentagon. As a friend of Laura's said, "It made her so sad seeing those guys wrapped up like mummies, trying to salute the Commander in Chief."

But Laura put her feelings aside in a statement to reporters. She praised the bravery and selflessness of the rescue team. She suggested that Americans could help in this crisis by giving blood. Again, she urged parents to comfort their children. "Let them know that most people in the world are good and this is a rare and tragic happening, but let them know they are safe and are loved all over the country."

Three days after the attacks, Laura, George, and his parents attended a memorial service for the victims of September 11 at the Washington National Cathedral. They understood that in a time of national grief, it is important for the country's leaders to guide the country in grieving. Former president Bill Clinton and Senator Hillary Clinton were also there, as well as former president Jimmy Carter and Rosalynn Carter, former president Gerald Ford and Betty Ford. The service was broadcast live on television, so that the whole nation could share it.

In the following days and weeks, Laura Bush gave several interviews on the radio and on TV. On *Larry King Live* she explained why she was stepping forward at this time. "Since September eleven I've had the opportunity, or maybe I should say the responsibility, to be steady for our country—and for my husband." Over and over, she talked about how important it was for parents to comfort and reassure their children. Keeping to a regular routine—"sharing meals together, reading stories before bed"—could be especially comforting.

Taking her own advice, Laura often called her daughters on the phone, or they called her. They chatted about everyday things, like the family dogs and cats. They made special efforts to be kind to each other. Barbara, at Yale University, called her father after his press conference October 11, a month after the disaster, to tell him how good he was.

It took a special effort for the Bushes to lead a normal life, because things were not normal. Security around the president is always heavy, but now it was even more serious. Snipers were stationed on the roof of the White House. Public tours of the White House had been canceled, something that hadn't happened since President Kennedy's assassination.

Visiting schools, Laura found the children she talked to very reassuring to her. "The most comforting people I've been with since September 11 are the second graders I've read to." She was deeply touched by the honest, heartfelt letters from children at schools she'd visited. "Dear

Mr. President," she quoted, "I love you. I love the firemen. I love the firemen's dog."

It became clear that the attacks on New York and Washington had been planned and carried out by *Al Qaeda,* a terrorist organization based in the Middle East. The leader of Al Qaeda, Osama bin Laden, was believed to be hiding in Afghanistan, but the government, called the *Taliban,* refused to give him up to the United States. President Bush ordered troops into Afghanistan to hunt down the terrorists.

To support her husband and her country, Laura Bush took a further big step into the public eye. On November 17, 2001, for the first time in history, the First Lady gave the president's weekly radio address. She wanted to help explain to the country, and to the world, why American troops were fighting in Afghanistan. She spoke about the plight of Afghan women, who were forbidden to go to school, work, or even leave the house by themselves under the ruling Taliban.

The Taliban were finally defeated, but the crisis didn't end there. Americans realized, more clearly than ever before, how open they were to terrorist attacks. There were so many ways to attack a country besides crashing hijacked planes into public buildings. That same fall, anthrax spores sent through U.S. mail (apparently not by Al Qaeda members) killed five people. This was just a small example of how deadly biological weapons could be. Also, people began to consider the possibility that water supplies for whole cities could be poisoned. Another danger was that nuclear plants could be blown up. The Bush administration responded to such dangers by launching a war on terrorism around the world.

Mrs. Bush explained in an interview how she was able to keep calm through the continuing crisis. There was her marriage, "a very sustaining relationship." There was her religious faith, which had been with her ever since childhood. Sometimes she worked out to calm herself down.

And she read. "I can lose myself in the book even when I'm anxious," she said. She was in the middle of a mystery novel, the kind of book that gave her some time out from real life. And as always, Laura comforted herself in a deeper way by reading great books like *The Brothers Karamazov*. They strengthened her faith that the very worst in human experience was not the final word about life.

In times of such great responsibility, Laura was happier than ever for George's big, supportive family. Doro Bush Koch and her husband, Robert, as well as Marvin Bush and his wife, Margaret, could often join George and Laura for weekends at Camp David, the presidential retreat in the mountains of northern Maryland. "That's very comforting for both of us, and very relaxing," said Mrs. Bush. "To laugh, to do all the things that brothers and sisters, family members who love each other, can do."

On Thanksgiving the Bushes gathered at Camp David with George's brother Marvin and his family and some White House staff members. They ate the traditional foods that Laura and George and their family had eaten for years: turkey with cornbread stuffing, green beans, mashed sweet potatoes, pecan pie. Some of the dishes, like the cornbread stuffing with sage, were familiar reminders of Laura's childhood. Laura liked to remember her father urging her mother, "Be sure to put in plenty of sage." And she liked to remember her father shelling pecans, from their own pecan trees, for Jenna Welch's pecan pie. Laura believed it was "really important, not just for Thanksgiving but other nights as well, for parents to prepare meals and have meals with their children."

In the summer of 2002, George W. Bush needed his wife's steady support more than ever. The U.S. campaign in Afghanistan had not succeeded in capturing Osama bin Laden or other key terrorist leaders. The world situation was grim, with Israel and the Palestinians locked in a cycle of violence and India and Pakistan threatening each other with nuclear weapons. Other countries expected the United States, the one superpower in the world, to keep the peace. But the United States was seriously considering attacking Iraq to overthrow the dictator Saddam Hussein.

President Bush's policies in the United States were not popular, either. Voters didn't approve of large tax cuts, now that there was a budget deficit. They also didn't approve of the Bush administration's push to allow drilling for oil in the Alaskan wilderness.

In the months following September 2001, the country had united behind President Bush with a burst of patriotic feeling. But by the spring of 2002, the big news story was not the September 11 tragedy—it was the recent scandals in the business world. Enron, WorldCom, and other corporations were being investigated for accounting fraud and other corporate abuses, and their stock value had plummeted. As a result, millions of Americans were left without enough money for their retirement. Investors lost faith in corporations' honesty, and the stock market plunged. Many people feared hard times ahead.

With business dishonesty so much in the news, President Bush's critics brought up old questions about his own business practices. They said that he had profited improperly from selling his stock in Harken Energy in 1990, just before the price of the stock dropped sharply. They said that in 1992 he and the other owners of the Texas Rangers had caused the city of Arlington to use hundreds of millions of taxpayers' dollars to build a new ballpark for the team.

It wasn't easy for Laura to hear her husband talked about that way. But she took this crisis as another opportunity to be "steady for my husband." She continued to promote her own causes, including reading and the preservation of historic places. At the White House, she decorated the walls of her office with pictures by N.C. Wyeth, a famous children's book illustrator. The bookshelves were stocked with children's books such as *Curious George* and *Little House on the Prairie*.

In June 2002 Laura Bush paid a public visit to the Orchard House in Concord, Massachusetts. There Louisa May Alcott had written one of Laura's favorite books, *Little Women*, in 1868. Speaking to an audience about preservation and reading, Laura asked to be introduced not as the first lady, but just as "Laura Bush" or "Mrs. Bush."

"Politics doesn't totally consume her," George had said of Laura during the campaign of 2000, "and as a result, it doesn't totally consume me." The girl from Midland, Texas, had been "Laura" all her life. She'd been "Mrs. Bush" for more than twenty-four years.

But Laura's stay in the White House will last only four years, or eight if George is reelected in 2004, and she doesn't consider it the most important part of her life. After the Bushes leave Washington, they will still have their pets, a stack of good books, and long walks on the ranch. They will have what Laura Bush really cares about: their family, their friends, and their home in Texas.

SOURCES

BOOKS

Bruni, Frank. *Ambling into History: The Unlikely Odyssey of George W. Bush.* New York: HarperCollins, 2002.

Bush, Barbara. *Barbara Bush: A Memoir.* New York: Scribner's, 1994.

Bush, George W., & Karen Hughes. *A Charge to Keep.* New York: Morrow, 1999.

Felix, Antonia. *Laura: America's First Lady, First Mother.* Adams Media Corp., Avon, MA, 2002.

Hatfield, James. *Fortunate Son: George W. Bush and the Making of an American President.* NY: Soft Skull Press, 2000.

Ivins, Molly, and Lou Dubose. *Shrub: The Short but Happy Political Life of George W. Bush.* New York: Random House, 2000.

Minutaglio, Bill. *First Son: George W. Bush and the Bush Family Dynasty.* New York: Random House, 1999.

Mitchell, Elizabeth. *W: Revenge of the Bush Dynasty.* New York: Hyperion, 2000.

Stone, Tanya Lee. *Laura Welch Bush, First Lady.* Brookfield, CT: The Millbrook Press, 2001.

MAGAZINE AND NEWSPAPER ARTICLES

Adler, Jerry, "Ground Zero." *Newsweek,* 24 September 2001.

Allen, Jodie T. "In Philadelphia, the Spouse That Scored." *U.S. News and World Report,* 14 August 2000.

Barnes, James A. "The Un-Hillary." *National Journal.* 28 April 2001.

Bilyeau, Nancy. "Meet the Next First Lady: Laura Bush." *Good Housekeeping,* October 2000.

Blyth, Myrna, and Nancy Evans. "Fighting for the Family." *Ladies' Home Journal,* November 2000.

Brant, Martha. "Don't Call Her an Adviser." *Newsweek,* 7 August 2000.

Brant, Martha. "The Steel Behind the Smile." *Newsweek,* 29 January 2001.

Bruni, Frank. "For Laura Bush, a Direction She Never Wished to Go In." *The New York Times,* 31 July 2000.

Burros, Marian. "Giving Thanks, at the President's Table." *The New York Times,* 14 November 2001.

Curtis, Gregory. "At Home with Laura." *Time,* 8 January 2001.

Gerhart, Ann. "Learning to Read Laura Bush." *The Washington Post,* 22 March 2001.

Grove, Lloyd. "Mrs. Bush Goes to Washington." *Harper's Bazaar,* June 2001.

Kastor, Elizabeth. "What You Don't Know (Really!) about Laura Bush." *Good Housekeeping,* September 2001.

Kornblut, Anne E. "Laura Bush Pursues Her Issues." *The Boston Globe,* 21 June 2002.

Kristof, Nicholas D. "A Philosophy with Roots in Conservative Texas Soil." *The New York Times,* 21 May 2000.

Levine, Ellen. "We Are All Changed. Every One of Us Has Changed." *Good Housekeeping,* January 2002.

Montgomery, Johnnye. "Breaking Up Is Hard to Do: Two High Schools in Midland." *Midland Reporter-Telegram*'s *The Ultimate High School Reunion,* June 2000.

Reed, Julia. "First in Command." *Vogue,* June 2001.

Schindehette, Susan and Richard Jerome. "Laura Bush: A Quiet Source of Strength." *People,* 9 November 2000.

Schindehette, Susan, et al. "What a Difference a Year Makes." *People,* 21 January 2002.

Schindehette, Susan, et al. "The First Lady Next Door." *People,* 29 January 2001.

Walsh, Kenneth T. "Laura's Moment." *U.S. News and World Report,* 30 April 2001.

Wildman, Sarah. "Portrait of a Lady." *New Republic,* 20 August 2001.

Winfrey, Oprah. "Oprah Talks to Laura Bush." *O: The Oprah Magazine,* May 2001.

TV AND RADIO TRANSCRIPTS

CBS Evening News, July 31, 2000, "Laura Bush Discusses Her Husband's Candidacy."

CBS Evening News, Oct. 18, 2000, "Talk With Bush Women on Campaign Trail."

CNN Programs, *People in the News,* "Laura Bush: Profile." April 8, 2001.

NPR News, *Morning Edition,* September 14, 2001. Interview by Bob Edwards, "Laura Bush Discusses What She Was Doing When the Terrorist Attacks Took Place and What's Ahead."

NPR News, *Morning Edition,* Sept. 4, 2001, Interview by Susan Stamberg, "Laura Bush Discusses Teaching."

NPR News, *All Things Considered,* July 30, 2000. Profile by Jacki Lyden of Laura Bush, wife of Governor George W. Bush of Texas.

NPR News, *Morning Edition,* July 31, 2001. Interview by Susan Stamberg, "Laura Bush on the Importance of Reading."

Washington Transcript Service, November 17, 2001. "Laura Bush Delivers the President's Weekly Radio Address."

WEB SITES

Midland, Texas, Chamber of Commerce Web site
(www.midlandtxchamber.com)

Texas Book Festival Web site
(www.texasbookfestival.org)

White House Web site
(www.whitehouse.gov/firstlady)